Philosophy
Sucks...
Kids Right In!

SmartFun Books from Hunter House

101 Music Games for Children by Jerry Storms

101 More Music Games for Children by Jerry Storms

101 Dance Games for Children by Paul Rooyackers

101 More Dance Games for Children by Paul Rooyackers

101 Movement Games for Children by Huberta Wiertsema

101 Drama Games for Children by Paul Rooyackers

101 More Drama Games for Children by Paul Rooyackers

101 Improv Games for Children by Bob Bedore

101 Language Games for Children by Paul Rooyackers

101 Life Skills Games for Children by Bernie Badegruber

101 More Life Skills Games for Children by Bernie Badegruber

101 Cool Pool Games for Children by Kim Rodomista

101 Family Vacation Games by Shando Varda

101 Relaxation Games for Children by Allison Bartl

101 Pep-Up Games for Children by Allison Bartl

101 Quick-Thinking Games + Riddles for Children by Allison Bartl

404 Deskside Activities for Energetic Kids by Barbara Davis, MA, MFA

Yoga Games for Children by Danielle Bersma and Marjoke Visscher

The Yoga Adventure for Children by Helen Purperhart

The Yoga Zoo Adventure by Helen Purperhart

Yoga Exercises for Teens by Helen Purperhart

101 Circus Games for Children by Paul Rooyackers

303 Preschooler-Approved Exercises and Active Games by Kimberly Wechsler

303 Kid-Approved Exercises and Active Games by Kimberly Wechsler

303 Tween-Approved Exercises and Active Games by Kimberly Wechsler

101 More Improv Games for Children and Adults by Bob Bedore

101 Comedy Games for Children and Grown-Ups by Leigh Anne Jasheway

101 Dialogues, Sketches + Skits by Paul Rooyackers, Bor Rooyackers, and Liesbeth Mende

Philosophy Sucks...Kids Right In! by Nel de Theije-Avontuur and Leo Kaniok

Philosophy Sucks...
Kids Right In!

Exploring Big Ideas
Using Small Tales from
Around the World

Nel de Theije–Avontuur
& Leo Kaniok

A Hunter House SmartThinking Book

An imprint of Turner Publishing Company

Turner Publishing Company
424 Church Street · Suite 2240 · Nashville, Tennessee 37219
445 Park Avenue · 9th Floor · New York, New York 10022
www.turnerpublishing.com

Library of Congress Cataloging-in-Publication Data
Theije-Avontuur, Nel de.
[Filosoferen met kinderen. English]
Philosophy sucks...kids right in! : exploring big ideas using small tales from around the world /
Nel de Theije-Avontuur and Leo Kaniok. — First US edition.
pages   cm
ISBN 978-0-89793-675-0 (pbk.) — ISBN 978-0-89793-692-7 (ebook)
1. Philosophy—Study and teaching. 2. Storytelling in education. I. Title.
B52.T4413 2013
107—dc23   2013029727

Project Credits
Cover Design: Jinni Fontana   Developmental and Copy Editor: Amy Bauman
Book Production: John McKercher   Managing Editor: Alexandra Mummery
Illustrator: Imke Meeusen   Rights Coordinator: Stephanie Beard
Publisher: Todd Bottorff

Printed and bound by Lightning Source Inc., La Vergne, Tennessee
Manufactured in the United States of America

9 8 7 6 5 4 3 2 1   First U.S. Edition   14 15 16 17 18

Contents

Preface

As the old Chinese saying goes: "A picture is worth a thousand words."

A story is also a picture but made of words; like brushstrokes, words form a metaphor, parable, or portrait. A good word picture may make a thousand other words superfluous. And like a picture, a story presents people with the opportunity to exchange ideas, each sharing what this or that piece says to him or her. And that is exactly the purpose of this book.

Children and adults all enjoy telling and hearing stories. Adults tell stories to children *and* adults; children tell them to adults *and* children. So why do we love to hear stories so much? What is the attraction? What's so special about stories? Is there even an answer to that question?

Perhaps we love stories because we discover things in them, and discovery is an adventure. When we hear or read stories, we never know in advance what we are going to discover, and that is the surprise. Life is a mystery, full of surprises and discoveries, just like stories.

Discovery is an interesting word. In the context of stories, it suggests "uncovering"; you remove a layer, and you can see what lies beneath it. A landscape is revealed—in this case an inner landscape—whether for just a moment or forever. And in this way, discovery and insight are closely related. If the covering is taken away, you can see what lies behind or beneath something, and you gain insight.

The German philosopher Johann Wolfgang von Goethe said *In der Kürze liegt die Würze*: "The essence lies in the brevity." He also said *In der Beschränkung zeigt sich der Meister*: "The master reveals himself through self-restraint." So much can be said in a few brushstrokes. A story is relatively short and limited, and it is precisely that which makes it a masterwork that brings across a simple but sometimes deep truth. A simple story may conceal a great discovery, and a great discovery may contain a simple truth. Reading or hearing stories is a journey of adventure. You may even discover something about yourself.

The collectors of these stories wish you an enjoyable journey.

— Erich Kaniok
Haarlem, The Netherlands, 2011

For easy reading, we have alternated the use of male and female pronouns. Of course, every "he" also includes "she," and vice versa.

Introduction:
Storytelling as an Approach
to Philosophizing with Children

Sharing stories from around the world, from all cultures and religions, is a great way of starting discussions with children about themselves, other people, and the world. You can use storytelling at school, in therapy situations, at home, or anywhere where you are working with children. The essence lies in talking with each other, thinking together, answering questions with new questions, and sharing thoughts and opinions. Children who participate in the storytelling experience learn from each other and grow.

The way in which the story is told is important, but still more important is the way in which the subsequent discussion goes. If the person leading the discussion is neutral and has an inviting manner, he is a philosopher in the true sense of the word—a "friend of wisdom" (this is the direct translation of the two ancient Greek words that comprise the word philosophy: *filos*, meaning friend, and *sofia*, meaning wisdom). The children experience the space for their own thoughts in an atmosphere that offers security and invites them to share their thoughts and feelings; an atmosphere in which it's not about knowledge but, rather, about exploring together. In this way, each child's input has value.

Why Philosophy for Children?

Philosophy stimulates independent thought. This means processing information, reasoning, creative thinking, evaluation. It promotes emotional development through self-knowledge, self-control, motivation, and the ability to empathize. This enhances children's social skills. It also helps with the discovery of large and small values, the universal and the local. It also helps with the search for purpose: "Who am I?" and "What can I mean in the world?" It helps with the development of a vision. Philosophy supports the feeling of "It's okay" toward one's own thoughts and opinions. Children have the right to ask questions, to form opinions, and also to change their minds. This is what helps children grow.

The process is beneficial to mentors too; philosophizing *with* children gives adults the chance to get to know the children better. It gives insight into how children think and feel about themselves, about other people, and about the world.

What Do the Stories Convey?

So, you will wonder, what do the stories in this book convey? Answering that question is the last thing we want to do. If we were to answer the question outright already, then we would have no reason to philosophize about it.

But what we can do is tell you about the stories. The stories have their basis in universal values such as happiness, love, friendship, peace, freedom, respect, justice, and equality. Each piece speaks about these matters in its own way. In that sense, each carries a message, often hidden in a metaphor, that can help in life whether now or far in the future.

The Stories and Discussion Papers

The stories included in this book are arranged by central theme, by underlying theme, and (for teachers) by links to the main aims and goals of education. This is not meant to limit the stories but rather to give suggestions as to how they can be used. We cannot emphasize strongly enough that what we have put in the discussion papers as Themes and Open Questions and Guidelines are only *possible options*, and you are invited to generate your own ideas. Tuning in to the children with whom you are working and adapting the questions for them accordingly is and will remain the most important thing.

How These Stories Fit with Present-Day Education

Stories have always been connected with education. Their content and form are constantly in a state of development—even today. Stories are closely connected with reality; they package it in an accessible and tangible form. The stories can be used for many purposes in education because they connect with every kind of goal. In this book we have limited ourselves to goals that are associated with social-emotional development.

Orientation on Self and the World—People and Society

In the area of social-emotional development and learning, children orient toward themselves and to how people relate to each other, how they solve problems, and how they find sense and meaning in their existence. They learn about the natural environment and about things that happen there. They focus on the world—close up and distant, then and now—and thereby make use of their cultural heritage.

How the Stories Fit in with Youth Work

Stories in this book act as mirrors, as many stories do. The details that children respond to in them say something about the children's self-image, their experiences, and/or their dreams for the future. This is true, in part, because a story offers readers the chance to first look at a situation from a distance. The discussion that follows the reading offers educators the chance to get close to the child, and for the child to get closer to himself.

Stories at Home or Within Other Environments

Stories form a connection, giving the adults the chance to get to know the children—and possibly themselves—better. Each story provides a strong starting point for fruitful discussions.

Directions for the Use of the Stories and Discussion Papers

The stories in this book, which have been rewritten especially for children, come from story collections from all over the world. We have also included some original stories for younger children. Wherever possible, we have mentioned existing books—mostly picture books—that present the same themes for younger children.

The Guide to the Stories

The table starting on page 6 gives a complete overview of the stories with age guidelines, themes, the developmental concepts being taught, and page numbers.

The Discussion Papers

Here we show you possible options—but you must remember to keep in tune with the children as individuals and the group as a whole to see what is most useful for the situation.

Which Stories Are Best Suited for My Group of Children?

The target audiences for individual stories are noted by age:

- children from 4 to 6 years old
- children from 6 to 8 years old
- children from 8 to 10 years old
- children from 10 to 12 years old

The central theme(s): What is the story about?
The underlying theme(s): What else does it convey?
The main educational goals of each story are listed under "Developmental Concept(s)" in the table starting on page 6.

Important Points to Consider in Advance

Think about the story. What does it say to you? Is it the right story for this child, for the group with which you are working, or for the class you are teaching? What can it mean to your audience? Do you think it will help these particular children think about what is significant and meaningful? Is it important in life, in this child's life, and in the lives of others? Talking about these ideas requires an atmosphere of safety and security, where the children can feel that their contribution is of value.

Ask yourself, "What is going on right now in the child or in the group you are working with?" Can you make connections between those things and the story? Where possible, find a way to connect with the children's own experiences. Does the story contain any elements that need explaining in advance? The questions in the discussion papers can offer a direction for the subsequent discussion in which you'll philosophize together about the story, but you'll certainly be able to find more questions that will apply to the story, the child, or the group.

Open Questions and Guidelines

After telling the story, be sure to make time in your reading session for the children's questions, their answers to those questions, and their ideas about the story in general. You should also make time to go through the Open Questions and Guidelines, which will lead the children to come up with their own thoughts about the story, about themselves and others, and about the world in which they live. And don't forget that they may have questions about the story as a story itself.

How the children process the story will differ in each case, each child, each group, and each situation. It is important to encourage each child to do this thinking in his or her own way.

Guide to the Themes and Developmental Concepts in the Stories

STORY	AGES	THEME(S)
"Just One Starfish" adapted from *Het geluk van Tao: verhalen en parabels uit Oost & West* [Keys to the heart: stories and parables from East & West] by Erich Kaniok and Leo Kaniok	6–12	Do what you can do whenever it's needed. Doing something is useful even if it feels like it's not enough.
"Two Crooked Boxes" by Nel de Theije-Avontuur	6–8	Self-image and judgment. Ways of looking at yourself. What do you see first: What's right, or what's wrong?
"Two Crooked Bricks" adapted from *Voorbij de woorden: boeddhistische verhalen en parables* [Beyond the words: Buddhist stories and parables] by Erich Kaniok	8–12	
The Rainbow Fish by Marcus Pfister (see References)	4–6	Give and take. Giving what you want to receive.
"The Poor Man and the King" adapted from *De taal van de stilte: verhalen en parabels uit Oost & West* [The language of silence: Stories and parables from East & West] by Erich Kaniok	6–12	
"The Cracked Pot" adapted from *Voorbij de woorden: boeddhistische verhalen en parables* [Beyond the words: Buddhist stories and parables] by Erich Kaniok	6–12	Self-confidence and self-appreciation.
Merry Christmas, Ernest and Celestine by Gabrielle Vincent (see References)	4–6	Peace. See the value of your own and others' contributions to peace, even if it seems to be a very small contribution.
"A Single Snowflake" adapted from *Het geluk van Tao: verhalen en parabels uit Oost & West* [Keys to the heart: stories and parables from East & West] by Erich Kaniok and Leo Kaniok	6–12	
Little Bear and the Echo (see References)	4–6	World view. Reflecting on the way you look at the world. Knowing your behavior can cause the same reaction in another.
"A Thousand Mirrors" adapted from *De taal van de stilte: verhalen en parabels uit Oost & West* [The language of silence: Stories and parables from East & West] by Erich Kaniok	6–12	

STORY	AGES	THEME(S)
"The Hungry Kaftan" adapted from *Sleutels tot het hart: verhalen en parabels uit Oost & West* [Keys to the heart: Stories and parables from East & West] by Erich Kaniok	8–12	Judging people by their appearances. Letting the first impression influence your contact with another person.
"The Three Caterpillars" by Nel de Theije-Avontuur	6–8	The freedom to choose your own path. Personal wisdom.
"The Three Frogs" adapted from *Het geluk van Tao: verhalen en parabels uit Oost & West* [Keys to the heart: Stories and parables from East & West] by Erich Kaniok and Leo Kaniok	8–12	
Duck and the Fox by Max Velthuijs (see References)	6–8	The danger of seduction and greed.
"The Calabash of Rice" adapted from *De taal van de stilte: verhalen en parabels uit Oost & West* [The language of silence: Stories and parables from East & West] by Erich Kaniok	8–12	
The Dawn Chorus by Ragnhild Scamell and Judith Riches (see References)	4–6	Respecting others and what they do. Living up to expectations or not.
"The Rooster and the Sun" adapted from *Het geluk van Tao: verhalen en parabels uit China* [The happiness of Tao: Stories and parables from China] by Erich Kaniok and Leo Kaniok	6–12	
Little Turtle and the Song of the Sea by Sheridan Cain and Norma Burgin (see References)	4–6	Freedom and feeling imprisoned. The influence of another person on that.
"The Circus Elephant" adapted from Erich Kaniok by Nel de Theije-Avontuur	6–10	
"The Tenth Donkey" adapted from *Sleutels tot het hart: verhalen en parabels uit Oost & West* [Keys to the heart: Stories and parables from East & West] by Erich Kaniok	10–12	

UNDERLYING THEME(S)	DEVELOPMENTAL CONCEPT(S)	PAGE
How important is one's appearance?	Gaining self-knowledge: the difference between being and appearance. Belonging or not belonging. Judging another person by his or her appearance.	44
Being yourself. The influence others have on your choices. The power of a group. What is real solidarity?	Self: taking on a challenge. Working together in a group. Positive and negative influence of a group. Group consciousness in relation to freedom of thought and action.	47
Not choosing greed over safety.	Healthy behavior: finding alternatives for risky snacking. Being aware and taking care of your own safety.	51
Considering group thought and individuality. The importance of asking questions. Doing your own task. Believing without thought.	Being unique and belonging in a group. Being independent in thought. Seeing your own limitations and capabilities. Working with integration and identity. Remaining critical of existing ideas. Respecting another's task.	55
What you think is true may not always be true, but it can still be a strong influence.	Examining self-image. Influence of limited experience. What is necessary for a positive, realistic image? Developing the freedom to think and do what you want, even while bearing others in mind.	58

STORY	AGES	THEME(S)
"Two Hedgehogs and One Worm" by Nel de Theije-Avontuur	4–8	Disagreements caused by the inability to share.
"The Boy and the Seagulls" adapted from *Het geluk van Tao: verhalen en parables uit China* [The happiness of Tao: Stories and parables from China] by Erich Kaniok and Leo Kaniok	10–12	Friendship and trust, self-interest, betrayal. Authenticity.
"The Teacher and the Stones" adapted from *Voorbij de woorden: boeddhistische verhalen en parables* [Beyond the words: Buddhist stories and parables] by Erich Kaniok	8–12	First take care of the important things in life. Less important or unimportant things distract you.
"The Ant and the Grain of Wheat" adapted from *Het geluk van Tao: verhalen en parabels uit Oost & West* [Keys to the heart: stories and parables from East & West] by Erich Kaniok and Leo Kaniok	6–12	Patience. Trust. Being able to let go or delay something for a purpose in the future. Trusting that a promise will be kept.
"The Reeds" adapted from *Voorbij de woorden: boeddhistische verhalen en parables* [Beyond the words: Buddhist stories and parables] by Erich Kaniok	8–12	The wisdom of flexibility as opposed to selfish rigidity. Being flexible.
"The Fisherman and His Wife" by the Brothers Grimm (see References)	4–6	Being happy with who you are. Becoming who you can be.
"The Stonemason" adapted from *Sleutels tot het hart: verhalen en parabels uit Oost & West* [Keys to the heart: Stories and parables from East & West] by Erich Kaniok	6–12	

STORY	AGES	THEME(S)
"A Different Chirp" by Nel de Theije-Avontuur	6–8	Misunderstandings that lead to quarrels. Language problems.
"Four Words" adapted from *De taal van de stilte: verhalen en parabels uit Oost & West* [The language of silence: Stories and parables from East & West] by Erich Kaniok	8–12	
"The Three Kittens" by Nel de Theije-Avontuur	6–8	Finding your place in the world. Considering the impression you leave behind.
"Signs on the Road" adapted from *Sleutels tot het hart: verhalen en parabels uit Oost & West* [Keys to the heart: Stories and parables from East & West] by Erich Kaniok	10–12	
Little Man Finds a Home by Max Velthuijs (see References)	4–6	Searching for happiness and forgetting to live. What is happiness?
"The Lucky Nut" by Nel de Theije-Avontuur	6–8	
"The Touchstone" adapted from *Sleutels tot het hart: verhalen en parabels uit Oost & West* [Keys to the heart: Stories and parables from East & West] by Erich Kaniok	8–12	Paying attention to what you have in your hands—what is there now.
Elephant and Crocodile by Max Velthuijs and Anthea Bell (see References)	4–6	Betraying trust. Seduction of riches. Wanting too much.
"The Young Bird of Prey" by Nel de Theije-Avontuur	6–8	
"Invisible Hunters" adapted by Nel de Theije-Avontuur from *De koning en de Indiaan: Verhalen uit Nicaragua* [The King and the Indian: Stories from Nicaragua] by Dick Bloemraad, Susan Breedijk, Fiona Macintosh, and Landelijk Stedenbanden Nederland-Nicaragua	8–12	
The Little Boy and the Big Fish by Max Velthuijs (see References)	4–6	Freedom. Second-guessing what another person wants from life, however well meant, can keep that person captive.
"The Bird" adapted from *Het geluk van Tao: verhalen en parabels uit China* [The happiness of Tao: Stories and parables from China] by Erich Kaniok and Leo Kaniok	6–12	

STORY	AGES	THEME(S)
"Jesse's Pet" by Nel de Theije-Avontuur	6–8	Limiting someone else's freedom by determining how he or she should be.
"The Displaced Eagle" adapted from *De taal van de stilte: verhalen en parabels uit Oost & West* [The language of silence: Stories and parables from East & West] by Erich Kaniok	8–12	
"The Horse's Three Questions" by Nel de Theije-Avontuur	6–10	Purpose of life, meaning of life. Recognizing what is asked of you right now. Taking responsibility.
"Three Life Questions" adapted from *Voorbij de woorden: boeddhistische verhalen en parables* [Beyond the words: Buddhist stories and parables] by Erich Kaniok	10–12	
"Grandfather Ant and Little Ant" by Nel de Theije-Avontuur	6–10	Learning from mistakes. Taking responsibility even outside your own territory.
"The Gardener" adapted from *Voorbij de woorden: boeddhistische verhalen en parables* [Beyond the words: Buddhist stories and parables] by Erich Kaniok	10–12	
Rosie and Roger by Rik Dessers (see References)	4–6	Dealing with your faults and the faults of others. Differences attract attention.
"The Five French Fries" by Nel de Theije-Avontuur	6–12	
"The Mole and the Mouse" by Nel de Theije-Avontuur	6–8	Everyone has their own reality, it is relative. Look beyond your own little world.
"The Wise Hen" adapted from *Het geluk van Tao: verhalen en parabels uit China* [The happiness of Tao: Stories and parables from China] by Erich Kaniok and Leo Kaniok	8–12	
The Bear and the Piglet by Max Velthuijs (see References)	4–6	Contentment. More stuff doesn't make you any happier. How much is enough?
"Little Hamster Never-Enough" by Nel de Theije-Avontuur	6–8	
"Contentment" adapted from *De taal van de stilte: verhalen en parabels uit Oost & West* [The language of silence: Stories and parables from East & West] by Erich Kaniok	8–12	

UNDERLYING THEME(S)	DEVELOPMENTAL CONCEPT(S)	PAGE
Self-image. Becoming yourself in spite of circumstances that might stand in the way. Finding your way through someone who believes in you.	Becoming/being who you are. Allowing another to be who he is, respecting another's self-image. Wanting and daring to accept help. Dealing with times when you do not know what you are or what you want (ages 8–12).	109
Doubting the purpose of life. Care. Respect for the insight and wisdom of another person.	Knowing what you are capable of, doing something with that, and being proud of it; self-appreciation. Dealing with doubt. Learning to respect and care for others.	112
The simplest way is not always the best. Stubbornly sticking to the same thoughts may stand in the way of finding solutions.	Operating from self-interest is not the same as caring about yourself. Daring to learn from mistakes. Daring to change your opinion. Being responsibile for completing a task.	117
Advertising makes use of human characteristics.	Healthy behavior: eating habits influenced by advertising. Dealing with your own faults and those of others.	121
Wanting to be right may come at the cost of truth.	Discovering what is important for you. Remaining open to what is important to someone else. In our multicultural society, getting to know many people can be enriching.	125
Learning to consider another's way of life.	Dealing with your own feelings of happiness or unhappiness. Dealing with contrasts in interests, opinions, and feelings. Thinking about your workload.	129

STORY	AGES	THEME(S)
"The King Who Wanted to Touch the Moon" adapted by Nel de Theije-Avontuur from *Magical Tales from Many Lands* by Margaret Mayo	4–6 (*If concretely illustrated*) 6–12	Selfishness: insisting on having things your own way.
"The Ladybug and the Lion" adapted from *Voorbij de woorden: boeddhistische verhalen en parables* [Beyond the words: Buddhist stories and parables] by Erich Kaniok	6–10	Respect through involvement. Valuing what someone has achieved in his own way rather than being condescending.
"The Emperor's New Clothes" by Hans Christian Andersen (see References)	4–6	Doing what other people tell you to do. Not wanting to change behavior even if it is wrong or senseless. Ignoring the wisdom of another person.
"The Millipede" by Nel de Theije-Avontuur	6–8	
"The Royal Calf" adapted from *De taal van de stilte: verhalen en parabels uit Oost & West* [The language of silence: Stories and parables from East & West] by Erich Kaniok	8–12	
"The Hissing Snake" adapted from *De taal van de stilte: verhalen en parabels uit Oost & West* [The language of silence: Stories and parables from East & West] by Erich Kaniok	8–12	Self-defense: standing up for yourself. Understanding when standing up for yourself becomes aggression.
"Light Goes with You" by Nel de Theije-Avontuur	6–12	Fear and trust: overcoming fear. Accepting help from someone else.
"Light Always Shines Ahead" adapted from *Het geluk van Tao: verhalen en parabels uit Oost & West* [Keys to the heart: Stories and parables from East & West] by Erich Kaniok and Leo Kaniok	8–12	
The Little Red Hen by Max Velthuijs (see References)	4–8	Sowing in order to harvest. Realizing your wishes. Doing something to make your wishes happen.
"Buried Treasure" adapted by Nel de Theije-Avontuur from *Stories from Around the World* by Heather Amery	8–12	

STORY	AGES	THEME(S)
"All Quiet in the Forest" by Nel de Theije-Avontuur	6–12	Wanting to be like another person. Imitating others can lead to a loss of self-respect.
"The Toad and the Goldfish" adapted from *Het geluk van Tao: verhalen en parabels uit Oost & West* [Keys to the heart: Stories and parables from East & West] by Erich Kaniok and Leo Kaniok	4–8	Talking, listening, and being quiet. The dangers of self-satisfaction.
"The Talkative Tortoise" adapted from *Voorbij de woorden: boeddhistische verhalen en parables* [Beyond the words: Buddhist stories and parables] by Erich Kaniok	8–12	
"Earthworms" by Nel de Theije-Avontuur	6–10	Greed. The pitfalls of greed: not being content with what you have, but always wanting more.
The Grouchy Ladybug by Eric Carle (see References)	4–6	You always have a choice as to how you react.
"Partridges" by Nel de Theije-Avontuur	6–8	
"In the Schoolyard" by Nel de Theije-Avontuur	8–10	
"Who Does It Belong To?" adapted from *Het geluk van Tao: verhalen en parables uit China* [The happiness of Tao: Stories and parables from China] by Erich Kaniok and Leo Kaniok	10–12	
Good Job, Little Bear by Martin Waddell and Barbara Firth (see References)	4–6	Equality: although they may appear different, in essence the big wave and the little wave are the same.
"The Little Wave" adapted from *Voorbij de woorden: boeddhistische verhalen en parables* [Beyond the words: Buddhist stories and parables] by Erich Kaniok	6–12	

UNDERLYING THEME(S)	DEVELOPMENTAL CONCEPT(S)	PAGE
Good cooperation comes from the contribution of each individual. Considering the role of a leader.	Self-respect: valuing your unique capabilities. Self-knowledge: also having insight into your own limitations. Cooperation in a group. Leadership.	161
Self-importance. Listening to good advice.	Self-knowledge: healthy self-appreciation. Healthy behavior: not losing sight of your own safety. Being able to listen means being open to the opinions of others.	165
Making use of seemingly weaker characteristics.	Understanding the addictive effects of something that you like. Learning the influences of that on behavior. The consequences. Seeing individuality in your behavior and that of others. Dealing with it.	169
Not allowing yourself to be influenced by others. Dealing with challenges and insults.	Dealing with conflict. Gaining self-awareness. Respecting each other. Reflecting on fights: prevention, causes, solutions. Dealing with group pressure and teasing.	172
Identity: self-knowledge, self-appreciation. Self-development: learning respect for individuality and individual abilities.	Expressing feelings, wishes and opinions. Recognizing your own capabilities, characteristics, limitations. Seeing equality in spite of differences.	179

The Stories

I can't save all the starfish, but I can save this one!

Just One Starfish

by Erich Kaniok and Leo Kaniok

The tide had just turned, and the waves, which had rolled far up onto the beach, had brought lots and lots of starfish with them. Now, as the tide began to ebb, each wave came a little less far up the sand. By this time, the water was no longer strong enough to pick up the starfish and carry them back to the sea, so they just lay there on the sand. Since starfish can't live without water, they were sure to dry out and die before the next high tide. The new waves would come too late.

Many people walking on the beach saw this happening, but only a small boy started picking up the starfish and throwing them back into the water.

"Why are you doing that?" one man asked the boy. "The ocean has thousands of starfish, and most of them are going to die anyway. What difference will it make if you save one or two?"

The boy looked at the little starfish floundering in his hand and then up at the man. "I can't save all the starfish," he said, "but I can save this one!" And he threw it back into the sea.

DISCUSSION

◉ The Story

"Just One Starfish" is suitable for children ages 6–12.

◉ Central Theme

You can't do everything, but if you do that one thing that you are *able* to do, it is worthwhile.

◉ Underlying Theme

Feeling powerless when too much is asked of you may lead to your doing nothing. Do what you can when it's needed.

◉ Developmental Concept

Social-emotional development: Knowing one's own abilities and limitations. What are you not able to do? What can you do? It is important that you do what you can—especially when it's necessary.

People and society. What do you do when called upon?

Managing powerlessness in certain situations.

Managing helplessness and dependence on others.

◉ Open Questions and Guidelines

For Children Ages 6–8

Why does the little boy take the starfish back to the sea?

What does the man think about the boy's actions?

Who do you agree with? Why?

For Children Ages 8–10

Begin with the questions that were used with children ages 6–8 and then add these:

Do you think more people will start throwing starfish back into the sea when they see what the boy is doing? Why?

Why don't other people do what the boy is doing?

Have you ever thought that something was "never going to work"?

Did you still try it anyway? Or did you decide not even to try?

What happened? How did that feel?

For Children Ages 10–12

Begin with the questions that were used with children ages 8–10 and then add these:

Have you ever felt powerless? Why? Did you still try to do something? Why? Why not?

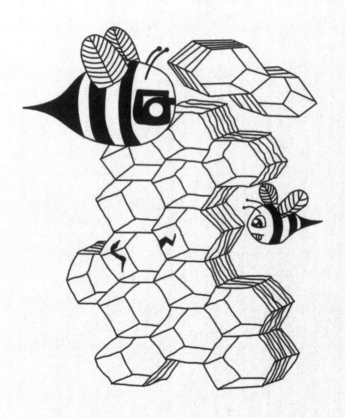

"Does this box have six equal sides?"

Two Crooked Boxes

by Nel de Theije-Avontuur

"Does this box have six equal sides?" Betsy buzzed cheerfully. "Let's take a look. Yes, that's right. Are they all exactly the same size? Yes, they are. And can we put the same amount in this box as in each of the other boxes? Yes. There, that's another one finished. Now for the last fifty."

"What kind of a riddle is this?" you may be thinking. If so, it might help to know that Betsy was a young bee who had just been taught to make honeycomb by the Great Honeycomb Master. Each box had to be exactly the same size with six sides that fit together so that the bees could keep honey in it.

The hive also had boxes where the Queen Bee laid her eggs. But you needed to be *very* skilled to make those. And that's just what Betsy wanted to be—an expert. She continued with the next box and the next one until she had finished the last fifty boxes. She was so happy to have finished the honeycomb!

She flew back a little way to admire her handiwork. "Oh, no!" she cried. "Two of the boxes are crooked!" Big fat tears rolled down her cheeks. "The big bees will be along soon to inspect my work, and they'll see that it's no good." Sadly she sat on the honeycomb, and she was still sitting there with when the big bees came along.

The Great Honeycomb Master was with them as well. "Whatever is the matter?" she asked.

Betsy buzzed tearfully, "Two of the boxes are crooked."

"Betsy, Betsy Bee," said the Great Honeycomb Master. "I can see 598 perfect boxes!"

"What?" Betsy asked. She looked again at all the boxes she had made. Now for the first time, she saw how many of the boxes were perfect. "My honeycomb is pretty good!" she buzzed happily.

The Great Honeycomb Master laughed.

Two Crooked Bricks

by Erich Kaniok

A man decided to build a house for himself, his wife, and their children. He wasn't a builder by trade and had never learned the skills to do it.

"Bricklaying looks pretty simple," the man thought to himself. "You put some cement on a brick, put it in place, and knock it in with the trowel."

Yes, it looked simple, but the man soon found that it wasn't. The man began laying the first row of bricks. But no matter what he did, they simply wouldn't lie straight. If they were straight at one end, they were all crooked at the other. Time after time he tried, over and over again. Even though he wasn't such a brilliant bricklayer, he was patient, and he worked on it until every brick was in place. Finally the first wall was finished. Feeling rather pleased with himself, he stepped back to look at his handiwork.

"Oh, no!" the man cried. To his great dismay he saw that two bricks were crooked. They looked awful and spoiled the whole wall. But by then the mortar between the bricks had hardened, and there was nothing he could do to set them straight. He called his wife to look.

"Should I break the wall down and start again?" he asked.

"No," said his wife. "Let it be just as it is."

So the man continued building.

One day someone came to see how the building was coming along. The man showed his visitor everything except the wall with the two crooked bricks in it. But the visitor walked around the whole building and saw that wall as well. "What a beautiful wall," he said.

The man looked at him in surprise. "Have you left your glasses in the car? Is something wrong with your eyes? Don't you see those two crooked bricks?"

"Yes," said the visitor, "I see two crooked bricks, but I also see 998 perfectly straight bricks."

The man looked at his wall in amazement. For the first time, he also saw the other bricks. Above and below those two crooked bricks, to the left and the right of them, all of the other bricks were perfectly aligned in a straight row.

DISCUSSION

◉ The Stories
"Two Crooked Boxes" is suitable for children ages 6–8.

"Two Crooked Bricks" is suitable for children ages 8–12.

◉ Central Theme
Self-image and self-judgment. When you look at yourself, what do you see first: what you like or what you dislike?

◉ Underlying Themes
Perfectionism. Self-image. Self-judgment. Judging others.

◉ Developmental Concepts
Social-emotional development: Knowing your capabilities and your limitations. Self-appreciation and self-consciousness. Recognizing that perfectionism can stimulate or hinder.

Community, norms, and values: Judging others.

◉ Open Questions and Guidelines
For Children ages 6–8, Relating to "Two Crooked Boxes"
Betsy only sees the crooked boxes. How do you think that happens?

Does the Great Honeycomb Master not see them? She mentions only all of the good boxes.

Have you ever had a situation when you tried to do everything perfectly and still something went wrong? How did that feel? Did you see only what went wrong, or were you also able to see what went right?

Do you sometimes see other people make mistakes? How do you react then? What do you do or say? Why?

For Children Ages 8–10, Relating to "Two Crooked Bricks"

The man first sees only the crooked bricks. How do you think that happened?

Why does the visitor see a "beautiful wall"?

Have you ever been in a situation in which you wanted to do everything perfectly and still something went wrong? How did that feel? Did you see only what went wrong or were you also able to see what went right?

Do you sometimes see other people make mistakes?

How do you react to them? What do you do or say? Why?

For Children Ages 10–12, Relating to "Two Crooked Bricks"

Begin with the questions that were used for children ages 8–10 and then add these:

The man's wife says, "Let it be just as it is." What do you think that meant to the man?

The man didn't want to show the visitor the wall with the crooked bricks in it. Why?

The man had seen only his faults and was blind to everything that went well. Has that ever happened to you?

Do you also like it when someone tells you that what you have done is good enough? Do you think other people would like that as well?

The Poor Man and the King

by Erich Kaniok

Once there was a poor man who felt he had been unlucky all of his life. That made him very sad. Every day he went to the market to beg for what he needed. "Can you spare a few cents for a poor man?" he would ask the passersby.

One morning he saw a golden coach driving into town. In the coach sat the king with a smile on his face.

Right away the poor man said to himself, "This is my chance! All that bad luck and poverty in my life is over and done with. The king is a friendly man, and he has come here just for me. I can feel it. He's going to give me a part of his riches!"

It seemed indeed that the king had come to the town especially for him, because the coach stopped right beside him. The man made a deep bow, stood straight, and looked the king in the eye and asked, "Can you spare something for a poor man?" He was certain he was about to have some good luck.

But the king stuck out his hand and said, "Can you spare something for me?"

The poor man didn't understand this. He was deeply disappointed. He didn't know what to say. "Do you think I'm crazy?" the man asked. "Are you making fun of me?"

He looked again at the king who was still smiling and still holding out his hand. Then the man put his hand into his bag where there was some rice. He took out a single grain of rice and gave it to the king. The king thanked the man, and the coach drove off.

At the end of the day, the poor man emptied his bag and found a single golden grain of rice. He burst into tears and sobbed, "If only I had given him all of my rice!"

DISCUSSION

◉ **The Story**

The Rainbow Fish, by Marcus Pfister (see References), is a book with a similar theme for children ages 4–6.

"The Poor Man and the King" is suitable for children ages 6–12.

◉ **Central Theme**

Give and take. Give what you want to receive.

◉ **Underlying Themes**

Stinginess. Wanting to receive but not wanting to give. Remaining dependent on others.

◉ **Developmental Concepts**

Social-emotional development: Sharing—being able to give and take. Mutual dependence of people and being independent.

Community, norms, and values: Welfare and poverty. Social obligations. Work.

◉ **Open Questions and Guidelines**

For Children Ages 6–8

Where do you think the golden grain of rice in the man's bag came from?

Why was there just one?

What do you think of the poor man? What do you think of the king? Why?

Do you sometimes give away things? Do you then want something in return? Why? Why not?

For Children Ages 8–10

Could the poor man have had a better life only if other people had given him a lot? What other possibilities were there?

If you had been the poor man, what would you have given to the king? Why?

If you had been the king, what would you have given? Why?

Do you sometimes give people things? Do you then want something in return? Why or why not?

For Children Ages 10–12

What do you think of the poor man's way of life?

Would you also have given the king just one grain of rice? Why?

Would you have given the poor man just one grain of gold? Why?

Can you imagine that some people have no choice but to beg for what they need? Do you know people like this? Where do they live? Why do they have to live that way? How does that compare to your life?

Do you sometimes give somebody something they need? Do you do it without wanting anything in return? How does that make you feel?

I am happy that you are the way you are.

The Cracked Pot

by Erich Kaniok

In the far off country of India, Narayani was walking to the river. She was carrying two pots to collect water for her mother. As she walked, she sang, and the pots swung in rhythm. One of the pots felt wonderful. It was very good at collecting water. The other pot was a little sad because he had a crack in his base. The pot thought, "Now I will be filled with water, but by the time we get home, half of it will have leaked out onto the ground. Narayani will have to walk to the river all over again."

The poor pot couldn't take it anymore. When they got to the river, he told Narayani what made him so sad.

"Oh, poor pot," said Narayani. "When we walk home, look at all the beautiful flowers along the path." The pot did what she suggested.

Seeing the flowers made him happy…until Drip! Drip! Drip! The pot felt the drops of water falling out of him.

Narayani saw that this made the pot unhappy. She said, "Don't you see? All the flowers are growing on *your* side of the path." And indeed the pot had not seen that, and he did not understand. "When I saw that you dripped, I planted seeds on that side of the path. Each time we pass, you water them. And just look at how many flowers have grown. I always pick a few for my mother, and she likes that. I am happy that you are the way you are."

DISCUSSION

◉ The Story
"The Cracked Pot" is suitable for children ages 6–12.

◉ Central Theme
Self-confidence and self-appreciation. Believing in yourself. Seeing your value.

◉ Underlying Themes
Being valued by another.

Accepting that you may have limitations and knowing that in addition to those limitations—or sometimes because of them—you have many possibilities.

Enjoying doing something for someone else.

◉ Developmental Concepts
When talking about sickness, handicaps, and health, you could discuss a temporary disability, like the crack in the pot.

Social-emotional development: Discovering one's own limitations and capabilities.

Developing self-esteem, self-confidence, self-awareness.

Understanding the limitations and abilities of others.

Community, norms, and values: Enjoying doing things for other people.

◉ Open Questions and Guidelines

For Children Ages 6–8

Why did one of the pots feel wonderful? Why was the other one sad?

Do you have times when things do not go right for you? How does that feel? And what do you do about those times?

Narayani tells the cracked pot that it is mainly because of him that the flowers along the path are blooming. Now that he knows that, do you think he will he still feel sad or will he feel differently?

For Children Ages 8–10

How do you think the undamaged pot felt about the pot with the crack in it?

How do you think the cracked pot felt about the undamaged pot?

Are you sometimes sad because you can't do something very well? What would help you in that situation?

Narayani tells the cracked pot, "I'm glad you are the way you are." What does she mean by that? How do you think the cracked pot reacted to her words?

For Children Ages 10–12

The undamaged pot was proud of himself. What do you think he thought of the cracked pot?

What did the cracked pot think of the undamaged pot? Why?

How do other people react when things don't go right for you? How do you feel about their reactions? Would you like other people to react differently? How? How do you react when things go wrong for someone else?

How do you react toward people who have injuries or handicaps that they have to deal with?

Narayani told the cracked pot, "I am happy that you are the way you are." How do you think the cracked pot reacted?

Do you have qualities about which you say, "That's just the way I am"?

A Single Snowflake

by Erich Kaniok and Leo Kaniok

A little brown wren sat on the branch of a pine tree. Around her it was snowing gently. Usually the little bird was busy, flitting here and there. Today she was still as a mouse. In the quiet, you could just barely hear her counting.

Counting? Yes, she was counting.

"And 3,997, 3,998, 3,999..." the bird said.

"What are you doing?" asked a voice.

The little wren almost fell off her branch in surprise. "Heavens above!" she said to the dove who was sitting on another branch of the same tree. "You made me jump. I didn't see you there. Have you been there long?"

"I've been here a while. In fact I've been here the whole time," said the dove. "I am the peace dove. I try to remind people that it's possible to have peace. But I have no idea what you are doing."

"I will tell you," said the wren, "but first I have a question. How much does a snowflake weigh?"

"I don't think it weighs anything," answered the dove.

"Then listen," said the wren. "Yesterday I was also sitting here counting. The whole branch was full of snow. I had counted up to 4,000 flakes, and they just kept falling...4,001, 4,002, 4,003, 4,004. Then flake 4,005 fell... and suddenly the branch broke! I fell to the ground in a heap of snow. So you can't tell me that that flake didn't weigh anything."

The dove was silent.

"I'm going to sit on another branch and start again because I've lost count," said the wren.

"Good-bye and good luck with your work," the dove called after her.

The dove sat thinking. "Could it be that a single snowflake made the branch break?" she said to herself. "If that's the case, could the same idea apply to peace? So many adults and children want peace. Could it be that it would take just one more person to join them for there to be real peace?"

DISCUSSION

● **The Story**

Merry Christmas, Ernest and Celestine, by Gabrielle Vincent (see References), is a story with a similar theme that could be used for children ages 4–6.

"A Single Snowflake" is suitable for children ages 6–12.

● **Central Theme**

Peace. Seeing the value of the contribution you and other people can make to peace.

● **Underlying Themes**

Anything a person says or does in the name of peace can contribute in some way to achieving it.

If we all want peace, it has a chance.

An individual's contribution to any cause is important.

● **Developmental Concepts**

Valuing your contribution to the whole.

Understanding that everyone can make a positive contribution toward a more peaceful society.

● **Open Questions and Guidelines**

The dove's question is the only real question for all groups: Could it be that it would take just one more person who wants peace and tries to live in peace for the world to have real peace?

Do you think so? Why? Why not?

Could that person be you? How?

What could people who want peace do together?

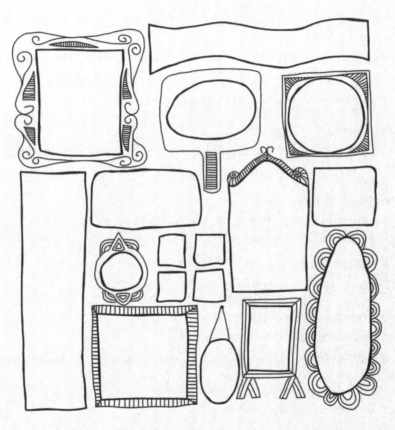

One of the attractions at the circus
was a tent with a thousand mirrors.

A Thousand Mirrors

by Erich Kaniok

A dog had heard that the circus had come to town. One of the attractions at the circus was a tent with a thousand mirrors. He really wanted to see that.

After a long walk, he came to the circus and found the tent. He looked for an opening where he could get in and, around the back, he found just what he was looking for. Once inside, he went through a couple of corridors, turned a corner and…suddenly he saw a thousand dogs looking at him from a thousand mirrors. This was fun! His tail started to wag, and the dogs in the mirrors wagged their tails as well. Thinking that the world was full of lots of friendly dogs, he decided he would go back every day to see them.

The next day, another dog came to the circus. He also visited the tent of mirrors, went through the corridors, came around the corner, and…suddenly, from a thousand mirrors, a thousand dogs looked at him. The dog was frightened; he bared his teeth and growled. The dogs in the mirrors also showed their teeth and growled back.

The dog jumped in fright and ran away with his tail between his legs, thinking that the world was full of angry dogs. He never ever came back again.

DISCUSSION

⦿ **The Story**

Little Beaver and the Echo, by Amy MacDonald (see References), is a book with a similar theme for children ages 4–6.

"A Thousand Mirrors" is suitable for children ages 6–12.

⦿ **Central Themes**

Reflect on the way you look at the world. Which "specs" are you wearing?

Your behavior can cause the same reaction in other people.

⦿ **Underlying Themes**

Going into the world with or without confidence. Learning the joy of meeting others. Exploring anger based on fear.

⦿ **Developmental Concepts**

Gaining insight into your own behavior and your behavior in relation to other people. Building self-confidence. Dealing with feelings.

Reflecting on conflicts: avoiding, causes, consequences. Dealing with mistrust and the fear of contact with others.

⦿ **Open Questions and Guidelines**

For Children Ages 6–8

The children can share their experiences.

Why did one dog wag his tail and the other one growl?

Is the world full of angry dogs or friendly ones? Have you ever been in a situation where you were really enjoying yourself and your attitude made someone else enjoy themselves, too?

Have you ever made someone grumpy or sad because you were grumpy or sad?

For Children Ages 8–10

As an activity, mirroring emotions can be a good way for the children to express what they experience when they see the emotions of another person.

What did you think or feel about this story? Can you explain why?

Why was one of the dogs afraid? How do you behave when you are afraid?

Why did the fearful dog growl? What else could he have done?

How do people react to you when you are in a good mood? How do they react when you are in a bad mood?

For Children Ages 10–12

What are you like when you feel at home somewhere and are enjoying yourself? How do other people react toward you then? How do you behave when you are uncomfortable and don't feel at home? How do other people react toward you when you feel that way?

Why is it that sometimes you don't feel safe or confident? What causes that? Being angry can sometimes be a useful reaction, and sometimes it is not. When might it be useful, and when not?

Do you ever feel aggressive if you are afraid or unsure? Does that make you feel less afraid and unsure?

How do other people react when you are angry? Do you know why they act this way?

The Hungry Kaftan

by Erich Kaniok

[NOTE TO THE LEADER: *It will help the children understand this story if they know that a mullah is a holy man in Islam and a kaftan is a kind of large robe with big wide sleeves but without a collar.*]

One day a mullah went to a feast given by an important person in the village.

When he got to the home where the feast was being held, he saw that everyone was wearing their best kaftan, made of silk or velvet. The other guests looked at him standing there in his simple clothes, stuck their noses in the air, and acted as if he didn't exist. They even pushed him away from the tables where the food was laid out.

"I know what to do about this," thought the mullah. He ran home, put on his most beautiful kaftan, and went back to the feast in all his glory. And then, like magic, all of the other guests could suddenly see him! Everyone wanted to talk to him. Suddenly he was the most important guest, and he was offered the finest delicacies from the table.

But instead of eating these fine morsels, the mullah put them in the sleeves of his kaftan.

"Mullah, what are you doing?" asked the other guests in astonishment. "Why do you not eat what we are offering you?"

When the mullah had stuffed his sleeves full of food, he answered, "I came here in my everyday clothes, and you couldn't even acknowledge my presence. You didn't offer me any food at all. But now that I am wearing my beautiful kaftan, you offer me more than I could possibly eat. And fair is fair. The food is clearly not for me but for my kaftan."

DISCUSSION

● **The Story**

"The Hungry Kaftan" is suitable for children ages 8–12.

● **Central Themes**

Judging people on the basis of how they look. Letting first impressions color the way you deal with another person.

● **Underlying Theme**

Appearances: Examining to what extent clothes make the man, woman, boy, or girl from both a positive and negative point of view. How important is outer appearance?

● **Developmental Concepts**

Social-emotional development: Gaining self-knowledge. Considering the difference between the inner self and the outer appearance. How important is the outer appearance in communication with other people?

Reflecting on judging another by his or her appearance. Do you still fit in when you are different, your clothing is different, or your way of behaving is different?

● **Open Questions and Guidelines**

For Children Ages 8–10

To the other guests, the mullah in his everyday clothes was different from the mullah in his fine kaftan. Why is that? What do you think?

How do you think the mullah felt in his everyday clothes? Do you understand that feeling?

How do you think the mullah felt in his fine kaftan? Do you understand that feeling as well?

The mullah gave the food to his kaftan. Why did he do that? What do you think about the mullah's actions?

Do you think the way someone looks is important? Is it important how you look? Why?

What do you hope that other people see when they look at you: how you look or how you are? Why?

How might the story continue?

For Children Ages 10–12

Begin with the questions that were used with children ages 8–10 and then add these:

Imagine that you were one of the guests at the feast. What would you have said or done when the mullah explained why he had given the food to his kaftan?

Can you give examples of people who stand out because of what they wear? What do you think about people standing out because of their clothes?

Can you give examples of people who are judged by other people because their clothes make them stand out?

The Three Caterpillars

by Nel de Theije-Avontuur

In a nest that appeared to be made from spiderwebs, a family of baby caterpillars crawled out of their eggs. They were hungry! Fortunately, that nest had been made in an oak tree, and little caterpillars just love oak leaves. They munched away until their tummies were big and round and the tree…was bare! Well, almost bare…but right at the top of the tree, at the tip of the longest twig of the highest branch, hung one more leaf. One leaf! All the caterpillars wanted a nibble of it, but it was so high that they were sure they couldn't reach it.

But three of the caterpillars thought differently, and they decided to climb the tree. Maybe they could reach it, they thought. And so they decided to climb higher. As they reached the bottom of the highest branch, all of the other caterpillars began to shout: "Don't do it! You'll never make it!"

One of the three caterpillars thought to himself, "They are probably right. I'd better not try." And he gave up.

The other two started to climb, but the crowd below kept on shouting: "Stop now!" and "It will all end in tears!" or "It's a dumb idea!"

Now the second of the caterpillars started to have doubts. "Maybe it's not such a great idea after all," he said. "If all of the other caterpillars say it's stupid, then they are probably right." And he lost his courage and stopped trying, too.

But the last caterpillar just carried on. Carefully he climbed all the way to the tip of that topmost twig. Finally he reached the leaf and started to nibble it. "Mmmm! Very tasty!" he said to himself. When he was full, he climbed back down the tree where all of the other caterpillars were waiting.

"What were all of you yelling about?" he asked the others. "I couldn't understand a thing you were saying. I think I may be getting a little deaf."

And the frog at the top?
He just stood there,
quietly enjoying the wonderful view.

The Three Frogs

by Erich Kaniok and Leo Kaniok

Three frogs wanted to hold a competition, so they decided to climb a mountain. All the local frogs came together to see it with their own eyes—and they all cried out, "That's never going to work! You don't even know how high that mountain is! Who on earth would try that? You know full well that it can't be done!" They all shouted their concerns at once.

The first frog who heard this decided that it wasn't worth even trying. If everyone was so sure it couldn't be done, then it must be true.

The other two frogs started to climb. And still the froggy crowd yelled to them, saying "Stop!" and "You know it's not going to work!" and "You're nuts!" Now the second frog began to have his doubts. So many frogs surely knew better than he did. They must be right, he thought. So he, too, quit.

But the third frog just went on climbing. After a long, long climb, he finally reached the mountaintop. The frogs down at the foot of the mountain just stared in amazement. And the frog at the top? He just stood there, quietly enjoying the wonderful view. He hadn't heard all the yelling and shouting—he was deaf!

DISCUSSION

◉ **The Stories**
"The Three Caterpillars" is suitable for children ages 6–8.

"The Three Frogs" is suitable for children ages 8–12.

◉ **Central Theme**
You have the freedom to choose your own path.

◉ Underlying Themes

Being yourself. The influence other people have on your choices and the power of groups. Being deaf to others in order to listen to yourself.

◉ Developmental Concepts

Gaining self-awareness. Knowing your own abilities and going your own way. Taking on a physical challenge.

Reflecting on the positive and negative influences of a group. Understanding group consciousness in relation to freedom of thought and action.

◉ Open Questions and Guidelines

For Children Ages 6–8, Relating to "The Three Caterpillars"

One of the three caterpillars didn't even start the climb, and another stopped in the middle of the journey toward the leaf. Why? Why did the third caterpillar reach the leaf?

What would you have done if you had been one of those caterpillars? Why? Have you ever tried something difficult? Did someone make a comment on your effort? What did he or she say, and how did that make you feel?

For Children Ages 8–10, Relating to "The Three Frogs"

The other frogs kept telling the three adventuresome frogs that their climb was a bad idea. Why? Why did the first frog give up so soon? Why did the second one give up half way? Why was the third frog able to reach the mountaintop? What do you think that the frog who reached the top would have done if he had heard the other frogs shouting? Why?

Have you ever done something that other people thought was not possible? What was that experience like?

For Children Ages 10–12, Relating to "The Three Frogs"

Begin with the questions that were used with children ages 8–10 and then add these:

Do you think that all the other frogs really agreed with each other? If you think they didn't, why did all of them shout out the same thing?

Have you ever given up on something you wanted to try because other people said you shouldn't do it? How did that make you feel? What is it like when other people encourage you to try something? Why?

Have you ever encouraged someone to do something? Why?

The Calabash of Rice

by Erich Kaniok

[NOTE TO THE LEADER: *Explain to the children that a calabash is a kind of big pumpkin. Tell them how, if there is a hole in the gourd, it is possible to put something in but not be able to take anything out with your hand.*]

In a clearing in the woods where the monkeys liked to play, there was a great big tree. In that tree hung a huge calabash, a kind of gourd, with sweet rice in it. A hunter had left it behind. There was a little hole in the calabash where the rice had been pushed in.

The calabash just hung there—but not for long, because a curious little monkey came along. First he carefully walked around the tree, climbed a branch not too far from the calabash, and had a good look. He thought it was a strange thing, but, oh, it smelled so delicious!

He crept a little closer and saw the hole where the wonderful smell was coming from. He could see the rice through the hole. He took the calabash in his hands, turned it around and around, sniffed it, and finally stuck his paw in the hole. He grabbed a handful of rice and.... Hey! Why couldn't he get his paw out any more? His fist, full of rice, was now too big to get through the hole. He became angry and screeched in fury.

Just then a tiger came along, and he was hungry. He heard the screech and just fancied a morsel of monkey. Did that monkey run away to safety? No, he wanted the rice and wouldn't let go of it.

You can imagine what happened...that greedy little monkey was eaten up. But how did that happen?

Was it the fault of the hunter who hung the calabash there?

Was it because the hole in the calabash was too small?

Was it because the tiger was hungry?

Or was it the monkey's own fault?

You tell us!

DISCUSSION

⦿ **The Story**

The Duck and the Fox, by Max Velthuijs (see References), is a story with a similar theme for children ages 6–8.

"The Calabash of Rice" is suitable for children ages 8–12.

⦿ **Central Theme**

Greed. Understanding the danger of greed and not being able to let go.

⦿ **Underlying Theme**

Not choosing greed over safety.

⦿ **Developmental Concepts**

Healthy behavior. Finding alternatives to risky sweet eating.

Social-emotional development: Being aware of and taking care of your own safety.

⦿ **Open Questions and Guidelines**

For Children Ages 8–10

The first questions are already found at the end of the story:

The monkey gets eaten. How did that happen?

Was it the fault of the hunter who hung the calabash there?

Was it because the hole in the calabash was too small?

Was it because the tiger was hungry?

Or was it perhaps the fault of the monkey himself?

What do you think?

What would you have done if you had been the monkey? Why?

How could he have eaten the rice without being eaten himself?

Have you ever been in a situation where something happened to you because you forgot to check that it was safe?

For Children Ages 10–12

Begin with the questions that were used with children ages 8–10 and then add these:

Why didn't the monkey let go of the rice?

Have you ever had a situation where you wanted something *so* much that you couldn't think of anything else? What happened? What was the result?

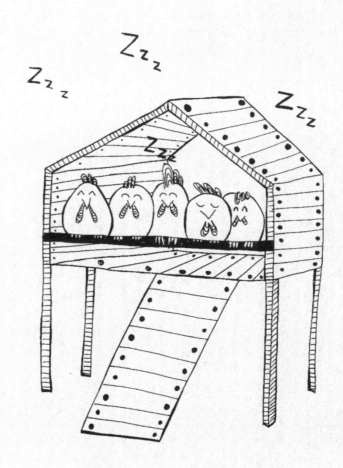

When evening came,
the chickens went into their
coop and tried to sleep.

The Rooster and the Sun

by Erich Kaniok and Leo Kaniok

On the chicken farm, the hens were all running around like mad things. The rooster was sick and couldn't crow!

"He has to crow tomorrow morning," said one hen, "otherwise the sun won't come up. If that happens, it will be dark all day long."

The hens clucked, and they bock-bock-bocked, but no one knew what to do. When evening came, the chickens went into their coop and tried to sleep.

When morning came, the rooster, sick as he was, hopped to the top of the compost heap. He threw back his head, opened his beak, took a deeeeeep breath, and…not a sound came out! Again he tried to crow, but again nothing happened. In the meantime, the sun came up, just as it always did—even without that rooster crow!

The hens watched in astonishment. Then they got very angry. All this time, they had believed that the rooster could call up the sun. "You're just a big cheat!" they said to the rooster, and they chased him away from the coop, out of the yard, and right off the farm.

In the evening, the sun went down, and the hens went to their coop as always. But the next morning when the sun rose again, they slept on. There was no rooster to wake them!

DISCUSSION

◉ **The Story**

The Dawn Chorus, by Ragnhild Scamell and Judith Riches (see References), is a book with a similar theme for children ages 4–6.

"The Rooster and the Sun" is suitable for children ages 6–12.

◉ **Central Theme**

Expecting more of someone than he is able to do, without seeing the value of what he is. Rejecting someone because he doesn't conform to the group's idea of what he is.

◉ **Underlying Themes**

Believing without thinking. Following group consciousness when it goes against the expression of individual opinions, wishes, and feelings.

The importance of being able or daring enough to ask questions. Doing what you can and carrying out your own task.

◉ **Developmental Concepts**

Social-emotional development: Being unique while still being part of a group. Developing independent thinking through which you learn to value your own wishes, feelings, and opinions as well as those of the group. Seeing your own limitations and those of another, and, while bearing those things in mind, seeing the possibilities.

Community, norms, and values: Considering the idea of belonging in a group, especially in regard to integration and identity. Being expelled from a group. Remaining critical toward existing ideas. Respecting another person's work.

◉ **Open Questions and Guidelines**

For Children Ages 6–8

What were the hens afraid of? Why? What do you think of the hens' fears?

What could the rooster not do? What was he able to do? Would you have chased the rooster away? Why or why not?

For Children Ages 8–10

Was it the rooster's fault that the hens thought he could make the sun rise? How do you feel about that?

Or was it the fault of the hens for the way they thought? In that case, how do you feel about that?

What do you think of the hens chasing the rooster away?

What was the important job that the rooster had?

For Children Ages 10–12

Do you think a hen might ever have come up with the thought: "Maybe it's not because of the rooster that that sun comes up"? What could that hen have done with that idea? How do you think the other hens would have reacted? Why?

Have you ever been disappointed because you believed something to be true and later learned that it was not true? How did that feel at first and how do you feel about it now?

Have you ever expected someone to do something that they couldn't really do—of your father or mother, for instance? How did you feel when you learned that that person couldn't do what you expected? How did you deal with it?

Do you think the hens were right to chase the rooster away? Why or why not? What was the rooster's real job?

The Circus Elephant

by Nel de Theije-Avontuur and Erich Kaniok

The circus music was building to a climax. Any moment Carlo the elephant was going to show off his best trick. All the other elephants sat obediently on their tubs. The trainer was standing by a huge tree trunk that Carlo was going to lift up and set down across two big tubs to make a bridge.

The tent was so quiet. You could almost hear the people thinking: "Can the elephant do that? Can he really pick up that heavy tree trunk? Surely he'll never manage that." The trainer gave Carlo a signal, and the elephant slowly walked forward, swinging his great head and flapping his ears. Once in position, he put his tusks under the tree trunk, threw his trunk around it and lifted the tree in the air. Carlo walked calmly toward the two tubs and set the tree trunk gently on top of them.

The audience burst into applause. Carlo gave a bow and went to sit on his tub. When the performance was over, a couple of children went with their parents to look at the animals. They saw the lions in their cages, the chickens that had been part of the clown's act, the horses, and the elephants. And there was Carlo. But now he had a chain around his foot, pinning him to the ground.

"Mama," said one of the children, "Carlo was able to pick up that heavy tree trunk. Surely he could pull that metal stake out of the ground—and then he would be free!"

"That's true," said the mother.

"Except he doesn't know that," said the father. "When Carlo was a baby elephant, they chained him to the same stake, which he couldn't pull out of the ground then. He still thinks he can't do it."

The Tenth Donkey

by Erich Kaniok

Once there was a farmer who had ten donkeys working on his land. After a long day of toiling and sweating, he took his donkeys back home and tied them to the rail that he had put up for that purpose. After tying up nine of the donkeys, he realized to his horror that he had lost the tenth rope. So he had nothing with which to tie up the last donkey.

What could he do? He was in a real fix! At that moment, the farmer saw a man resting under a tree a little way off. He went up to him and said, "May I ask you something?"

"Of course," said the man. "What can I do for you?"

The farmer explained his problem.

"Well, I don't have any rope, but I do have an idea," said the man. "All you need to do is to make the movements you would make if you actually had a rope. Pretend to tie the donkey to the rail. It's as simple as that."

The farmer went back to the tenth donkey, pretended to tie a rope around his neck, and tie it to the rail. After that, he went into his house. He wanted to trust the strange advice the man had given him, but he was worried that in the dead of night his tenth donkey would wander away.

The next day, when he stepped into the morning sunshine, he saw that all the donkeys were standing obediently at the rail—even the tenth donkey. Happy that everything had gone so well, he untied the nine donkeys and wanted to take them to the field to work. To his surprise, the tenth donkey refused to move. The farmer pulled and pushed him, but the animal just stood where he was and wouldn't move.

Then he looked to the tree where the man had been sitting the previous day. The man was sitting there again. The farmer walked over to him and told him what was going on, at which point the man asked, "But have you untied the tenth donkey?"

"No, of course not," said the farmer. "He isn't really tied up at all!"

"Aha!" said the man, "You see, *you* know that the donkey isn't tied up, but the donkey doesn't know that. He still thinks he's tethered to the rail!" The farmer went back to the donkey and pretended to untie a rope and remove it from around the animal's neck. He had hardly finished when the donkey walked off to join the others and went with them to the field.

DISCUSSION

◉ The Stories
Little Turtle and the Song of the Sea, by Sheridan Cain and Norma Burgin (see References), is a story with a similar theme for children ages 4–6.

"The Circus Elephant" is suitable for children ages 6–10.

"The Tenth Donkey" is suitable for children ages 10–12.

◉ Central Theme
Freedom and the feeling of imprisonment. Examining the influence another person can have on your feeling of freedom.

◉ Underlying Theme
What you think is true may not always be true, but it can still be a strong influence.

◉ Developmental Concepts
Examining self-image. Experiences of limitation can remain an influence for a long time. What do you need to have a positive, realistic image?

Learning about coexistence. Developing the freedom to think and do what you want even while remaining aware of other people. And, on the contrary, examining the idea of *not* having that feeling of freedom.

◉ Open Questions and Guidelines
For Children Ages 6–8, Relating to "The Circus Elephant"
Carlo is a big strong elephant, and yet he doesn't realize that he could pull out the stake that pins him to the ground. The children's father explains why Carlo doesn't pull out the stake. Do you think his explanation is correct?

Do you think Carlo would want to leave the circus? Why or why not?

Are there things you think you can't do or aren't allowed to do? Why?

Would you want to try any of those things?

For Children Ages 8–10, Relating to "The Circus Elephant"

Begin with the questions that were used with children ages 6–8 and then add these:

Can you do everything you want to do? Why or why not?

For Children Ages 10–12, Relating to "The Tenth Donkey"

Why does the tenth donkey not wander away even though he is not tethered to the rail? How did that happen?

The donkey thinks that he's not able to do something. Do you feel the same way sometimes? When? Are you sure that you can't do it? Would you want to try it anyway?

Can you do everything you want to do? Why or why not?

What makes people feel that they are not free to think or do what they want to?

Have you had that experience yourself?

Two Hedgehogs and One Worm

by Nel de Theije-Avontuur

One lovely Sunday morning, it was still quiet in the garden. The first birds were just starting to sing. Two hedgehogs, who were the best of friends, were on their way to their hideaway under a pile of twigs. They had been out all night and were ready to sleep. Then one of the hedgehogs saw a big, fat worm pop its head out of the ground. He said nothing but just dawdled a bit until his friend had almost disappeared under the twigs. Then he trotted off to the place where he had seen the worm as quick as his legs would carry him.

In the meantime, his friend had noticed that he was all alone. As he turned around, he saw the worm, too! He also wanted to eat it. He ran toward the worm, shouting, "It's my worm! I saw it first!"

The other hedgehog turned around and shouted back, "That's what you think! You weren't even looking. You can't have seen it before I did!"

"Yes, I did."

"No, you didn't!"

"Yes, I did!"

"No, you didn't!"

"Yes, I did,"

"No, you didn't…"

And so they went on.

And the worm? Well, he had already gone back down into his burrow. When the hedgehogs finally stopped arguing, they saw that the worm had gone.

"This is all your fault," said one.

"No, it wasn't!" said the other.

And off they went again, back and forth. Well, finally they were tired out, and they each went off to find a sleeping place by himself. Their usual burrow under the pile of twigs stayed empty. They slept all day long, and when the sun started to set, the first hedgehog woke up all alone. He scuttled out from under the heap of leaves and…almost tripped over half a worm.

Who do you think could have put it there?

DISCUSSION

◉ **The Story**

"Two Hedgehogs and One Worm" is suitable for children ages 4–8.

◉ **Central Theme**

Disagreements caused by the inability to share.

◉ **Underlying Themes**

Having a friendship, being alone, making up when friends fight.

◉ **Developmental Concepts**

Learning the value of friendship. Fighting with people who are close to you.

Making your own choices, seeing the consequences of your actions, and making up when those choices lead to disagreements.

Exploring the idea of sharing with others and learning that friendship requires a lot of sharing.

◉ **Open Questions and Guidelines**

What do you think of the hedgehog who didn't tell his friend that he'd seen a tasty worm? Why?

What do you think of the hedgehog who said that he'd seen the worm first? Why?

What would you have done if you had been one of those hedgehogs? Why?

How could both hedgehogs have gotten something to eat and still remained friends?

Who do you think left that half of worm for the first hedgehog?

The story is not finished yet. What would you like to add to it?

*It would be really easy
to catch a couple of these seagulls.*

The Boy and the Seagulls

by Erich Kaniok and Leo Kaniok

There once was a boy who loved seagulls. Every morning he rowed his boat into the ocean, and at least a hundred seagulls would follow him.

When he was far from the shore, he would stop rowing and lie down on the floor of the boat to watch the birds. They circled above his head, gliding through the air. They dived around him, catching fish. They came and sat on the side of the boat to rest. Sometimes one or two even sat on his shoulders. The boy and the seagulls played games with each other; he would throw pieces of bread into the water to see which bird got there first, or the gulls would drop fish they had just caught into the boat and try to pick them up again before the boy got to them.

But one day everything changed. That was the day the boy thought, "It would be really easy to catch a couple of these seagulls. I'm sure someone would be very pleased to have one. Maybe I even could sell them."

That day, when he rowed out to sea, the seagulls followed him as usual. He lay down in the boat as he always did. And the gulls—they flew in circles high above his head, but they didn't land on the boat. They picked the bread out of the water but didn't drop their fish into his boat...and none of them sat on his shoulders.

◉ **The Story**

"The Boy and the Seagulls" is suitable for children ages 10–12.

◉ **Central Themes**

Friendship. Friendship and trust, self-interest, betrayal.

◉ **Underlying Themes**

Good or bad intentions. People and animals feel not only what you do or say but also what your intentions are.

◉ **Developmental Concepts**

Social-emotional development: Developing friendships, an awareness of others, and an awareness of your own wishes. Feeling and understanding how something is intended.

Community, norms, and values: Understanding the characteristics and expressions of friendship.

◉ **Open Questions and Guidelines**

For Children Ages 10–12

At the start of the story, the seagulls came very close to the boy. Why?

Why did they not approach him later in the story?

How obvious are a person's wrong intentions, such as telling lies or planning something that they shouldn't be planning?

Have you ever had someone know you were planning something you shouldn't be planning? What happened and how did you feel?

Have you ever "seen" or "felt" that someone else was planning or doing something wrong? What happened and how did you feel about that?

Who do you think the boy was thinking of most when he had the idea of catching some seagulls? Why do you think that? Do you recognize that from your own experience?

If you had been one of the seagulls, how would you have felt?

How do you think the rest of the story went? What would the boy have done?

How would the seagulls react?

The Teacher and the Stones

by Erich Kaniok

At school, a group of students were waiting for the teacher. What would he have to tell them today? At last he came in, carrying a big bag.

"Good morning, everyone," he said.

"Good morning," said the students. And then one of them called out, "What have you got in that bag?"

"You're very curious," said the teacher, "but you're in luck because I'm just about to show you."

He put a glass vase on his desk and pulled a handful of stones out of his bag. He put the stones carefully into the vase one by one until it was full. "Is the vase full?" he asked the group. The students all thought that it was. The teacher smiled and took a jar of pebbles from the bag. He threw these little stones on top of the larger ones and by shaking it gently, the pebbles dropped down into the gaps.

"Is the vase full now?" he asked the class. Most of the students thought it was, although you could see that one or two were pondering on the question. "…or not?" They saw the teacher smiling again. He took a jar of sand from the bag, threw the sand in the vase, shook it a little, and all the sand dropped through between the stones and the pebbles.

"Is the vase full?" Now all the students thought there couldn't possibly be room for anything more, but from the teacher's grin they could see there was still another part to the story. And so there was; the teacher took a jug of water and emptied it into the vase. "NOW the vase is full!" he said. "But watch; we're going to do this another way. I have another vase just the same size, an equal number of stones and pebbles, the same amount of sand and water—but this time we're going to start with the water, then the sand, then the pebbles, and finally the stones."

With the help of a couple of students, they put the water, the sand, and the pebbles in the vase, but when it came to the larger stones, to their amazement, they wouldn't all fit in. The teacher asked the group, "Who wants to say something about what we just saw?"

[NOTE TO THE LEADER: *Try asking the question of the children. "Who wants to say something about what we just heard? One of you, perhaps?"*]

Maybe it would be a good idea to re-enact the story. Re-enacting it will show it concretely, letting the children experience it and giving them the opportunity to draw parallels between the story and their own lives. If you decide to do this, don't read the next paragraph, as too much will already have been explained.]

One of the students said, "When the biggest stones go in last, they can't get in between the other things in the vase. Do the big things always have to go in first, then?"

The teacher said, "If this vase represented your life, what are the big stones?" Together they came to the conclusion that the large stones represented the most important things in life; the people you love, family and friends; the person you really want to be; the things that are most valuable to you; the things you most want to give your time and attention to. "As long as you give the most important things in your life first place, there will always be enough space for other things," said the teacher.

DISCUSSION

● **The Story**

"The Teacher and the Stones" is suitable for children ages 8–12.

● **Central Theme**

First, do the things in your life that are the most important. Less important or unimportant things distract you.

● **Underlying Theme**

Learning to understand and respect what another person finds important.

● **Developmental Concepts**

Every person is unique and searching for what is important to him or her in life.

For different people, different things may be important. Recognize that, find out more about it, and bear it in mind.

● **Open Questions and Guidelines**

For Children Ages 8–10

See the conclusion of the story.

What is important to you?

Do you sometimes do the less-important things first and only later give attention to the important things?

What do your classmates find important? What is important to your father or mother? Do they find other things more important than those things that are important to you? Can you understand that?

For Children Ages 10–12

See the conclusion of the story.

Begin with the questions that were used with children ages 8–10 and then add these:

Do you want your close friends to list as important the same things that you find important? Why or why not?

Do you know people who value completely different things? Do you understand that?

How can you learn to understand them?

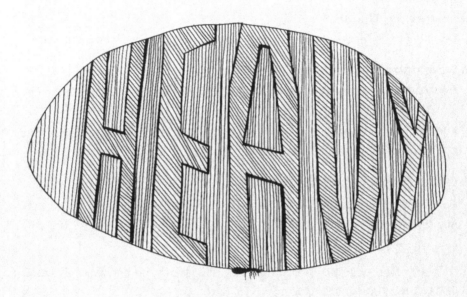

Hundreds of grains
in exchange for a single grain?
That sounded like a miracle.

The Ant and the Grain of Wheat

by Erich Kaniok and Leo Kaniok

After the harvest, there was a single grain of wheat lying in the field. It was waiting for the rain to make the dry soil around it get muddy. After that, it would sink in, form roots, and start to grow.

But before this could happen, along came an ant. The ant saw the grain of wheat and, with a huge effort, hoisted it onto his back and began the long journey back to the anthill.

It wasn't easy. The weight of that grain of wheat on his little body became heavier and heavier.

"Why are you bothering with all that lugging about? Why don't you just put me down?" asked the grain of wheat.

The ant panted, "If I don't take you with me, we will have less food for the winter. I live with many, many other ants, and we all have to bring food home to the storeroom."

"But I'm not created to be eaten that way!" said the grain, "I am a seed, full of life. I'm made to grow into a new big ear of wheat. Listen to me, and let's decide together what to do."

The ant was happy that he could take a little rest. He put the grain down and asked, "What do you want to explain to me?"

The grain said, "If you leave me here in the field instead of dragging me off to your nest, then I'll give you hundreds of grains for your storeroom!"

The ant thought about it. Hundreds of grains in exchange for a single grain? That sounded like a miracle. "How could that happen?"

"That's a secret," said the grain. "That is one of life's great secrets. Dig a little hole in the ground, drop me in, and come back in a year's time."

A year went by, and the ant came back. And the grain of wheat? He was as good as his word.

◉ **The Story**

"The Ant and the Grain of Wheat" is suitable for children ages 6–12.

◉ **Central Themes**

Patience, trust. Being able to let go now and hang on for a greater goal. Believing that a promise will be fulfilled. Being trustworthy. The ant trusts that the grain of wheat will fulfill its promise, and it does.

◉ **Underlying Themes**

The purpose of life; the secret of new life. Understanding that from a tiny seed a big, new plant will grow.

Working in the interest of living with others.

◉ **Developmental Concepts**

Taking care of yourself and caring for others. The grain wants to fulfill the purpose of its life. Meanwhile, each of the ants in the anthill have a task in caring for the others, such as, collecting food.

Considering the purpose of your life as part of the larger community; considering the interests of others.

Community, norms, and values: Seeing the division of tasks in the anthill as representing the idea behind community. Sticking to agreements. Trusting one another.

◉ **Open Questions and Guidelines**

For Children Ages 6–8

What does the ant want? For whom? Why?

What does the grain of wheat want? Why?

What does the grain of wheat mean when it says, "That is one of life's secrets"?

The ant and the grain of wheat make an agreement. The ant trusts that the grain will stick to the agreement. What would you have done?

The grain of wheat was true to his word. Do you know how?

For Children Ages 8–10

What does the ant want? For whom? Why?

What does the grain of wheat want? Why?

The grain wants to make an agreement. What does the ant do? What would you have done?

How could the grain of wheat stick to the agreement?

Do you sometimes make promises to other people? Do you keep them?

For Children Ages 10–12

The ant and the grain each have a purpose in life. What is the grain's purpose? What is the ant's purpose?

The ant trusts the promise made by the grain of wheat: "If you leave me here in the field, then I'll give you hundreds of grains for your storeroom!" What would you have done? Why?

How did the grain keep its promise?

Do you sometimes make promises? Do you keep them?

What kind of things do you do mainly for yourself? What do you do mostly for others?

In India, after a long, winding journey,
the River Ganges flows into the ocean.

The Reeds

by Erich Kaniok

In India, after a long, winding journey, the River Ganges flows into the ocean.

"There is something I don't understand," said the ocean to the river, "When it rains very hard, you get bigger, stronger, more furious. Then you drag many things with you—even whole tree trunks! But I never see grass, or a reed stalk, or a tuft of reed. Why not? Are they not worth it for you? Are they too weak?"

The Ganges said, "I will explain it to you, Ocean. The grass and the reeds don't remain stiff. They bend with the current. If I flow over them, I can push them down, but I can't tear them out of the ground because they move with me, so I can't take them with me. They know how strong I am, and they don't try to oppose that. If I flow more gently, they stand in their own spot and continue to grow. But the trees—that is another story altogether. They just stand stiffly and don't bend when the waves come, so they bear the full brunt of my power, and they break. And that is how I carry the larger and mightier trees to you but leave the grass and the reeds where they stand, even though they are much less strong."

"Aha, I think I understand," said the ocean.

DISCUSSION

◉ **The Story**
"The Reeds" is suitable for children ages 8–12.

◉ **Central Theme**
Bending or breaking; being flexible. The wisdom of remaining flexible rather than rigid.

◉ Underlying Theme

When something happens to you, resistance is of little help. Becoming part of it, or using it can help a lot. Recognizing and accepting stronger forces.

◉ Developmental Concepts

Healthy behavior: Choosing survival and going with the flow.

Knowing your own capabilities and limitations. Knowing you have limits.

Social-emotional development: Accepting dependence.

Going with the flow as a choice at a particular moment.

Dealing with group pressure. Daring to think differently; daring to react differently.

◉ Open Questions and Guidelines

For Children Ages 8–10

Why did the trees fall?

Why did the smaller plants remain standing?

Do you think that the river paid attention to the plants that were less strong?

Do you know what things you are not (yet) strong enough to do? Do other people bear that in mind?

Do you bear in mind that other people may not be as strong as you are?

Have you ever had something happen to you that you didn't want? What did you do? Did it help? Would it have been better if you had done something else?

For Children Ages 10–12

Begin with the questions that were used with children ages 8–10 and then add these:

Do you think that the smaller plants are weak and offered too little resistance?

The smaller plants chose to let the river flow over them. What do you think about that?

The trees chose to stand up stiffly. What do you think about that?

Do you sometimes react like the trees or are you more like the plants?

Could you come up with another title for this story?

The Stonemason

by Erich Kaniok

Once upon a time, there was a stonemason who worked every day in the mountains. Today, just as every other day, he was working, and he had gathered almost enough rock to sell. Chip chip, chop…it became like a song. It cheered him up, and he was happy. He enjoyed his work and often said of his life, "I have enough to eat and a nice hut to live in."

The next day, the stonemason was working for a rich man who had a beautiful house and a wonderful garden. A big rock blocked the view of the garden from the house and had to be removed. It was the stonemason's job to chop the rock into small pieces and take them away. He chipped away. Chip…chop…chip! It made him tired…chop, chip… and then, suddenly, he couldn't hear anything.

The stonemason gazed at the house and thought, "Why should I have to work so hard? I would like to be rich and have a beautiful house with a garden."

"All right," a voice said, as if in answer to his thoughts. "Your wish is granted. From now on, all your wishes will be fulfilled."

The stonemason dropped his tools in amazement. Who had said that? Confused and a little afraid, he picked up his tools and headed home. When he got there, though, he saw that what the voice had said was true. His little hut had vanished, and in its place stood a very beautiful house in the midst of a wonderful garden. He was rich! "I don't need to work anymore!" he cried happily.

For a long time, the man was happy in his new house. Then, one lovely warm day, the king came by in his coach. "Oh, it must be lovely and cool in that coach," the man said to himself. "It's so hot here in the house. I wish that I were the king."

"No sooner said than done," a voice said. "Your wish is granted."

And there he was, like a king, in the coach. Unfortunately, it wasn't at all cool inside the coach. "Pffff!" the man snorted. "I can't believe the sun can get in here and make it so hot! In that case, I wish that I were the sun!"

Once again, his wish was granted. He became the sun and sent hot rays down to the earth. Everything went fine until a thick cloud came and hung in front of him. He wanted to shine through the cloud, but he just couldn't do it. "Humph! That great cloud can get in my way? Well, in that case, I wish I were a cloud!"

And so it happened. He became a cloud. A rain cloud. But, as you know, out of a rain cloud comes…rain! He fell in drops and dribbles back to the earth. As a matter of fact, the rain fell on a mountain, and there the drops came together and flowed lower and lower down the mountain until they came to a great block of rock.

The rain couldn't go through the rock, and it couldn't go under the rock, so it had to flow all the way around it.

"Is that rock so strong? Well, in that case, I think I'd like to be a rock!" And, yes, before he knew it, he was lying on the mountain as a stone. He was a huge block of rock. Then he heard something: Chip, chip, chop! Chip, chip, chop! He looked around him, and he saw a man chopping bits off of him with a hammer and chisel.

"What!" he cried. "Such a small man can chop me into little bits? I'd like to be a man like that!"

"Your wish is granted!"

And so he became a stonemason and worked every day in the mountains. And every day he happily sang his song.…

DISCUSSION

⊙ **The Stories**

"The Fisherman and His Wife," by the Brothers Grimm (see References), is a story with a similar theme for children ages 4–6.

"The Stonemason" is suitable for children ages 6–12.

⊙ **Central Themes**

Being happy with who you are. Being who you can be.

⊙ **Underlying Themes**

Longing for something someone else has or can do may prevent you from being happy and content.

Longing for power.

⊙ **Developmental Concepts**

The unity of all people.

Understanding self-knowledge, self-development, self-esteem. Expressing feelings and longings. Dealing with your own capabilities, limitations, and wishes.

Valuing your own part in the community; valuing the part of others as well.

⊙ **Open Questions and Guidelines**

For Children Ages 6–8

At the start of the story, the stonemason is content. What does it mean to be content? Do you feel content sometimes? Why or why not?

Why does the stonemason want to be someone else?

At the end of the story, he is a stonemason again, and he is content once more. How did that happen?

What would you have done if you were the stonemason?

For Children Ages 8–10

Begin with the questions that were used with children ages 6–8 and then add these:

Do you sometimes feel like the stonemason? When?

Do you wish you were someone else? Why? Do you want something someone else has? Why?

Are you happy with something you can do, something you have, something you are?

For Children Ages 10–12
Begin with the questions that were used with children ages 8–10 and then add these:

What is it that the stonemason really wants each time?

Would it be good if you could be someone or something that you are not? Why or why not?

Do you know people who are content with who they are, what they have, and what they do? How do you feel about that kind of contentment?

In the beginning and at the end of the story, the stonemason is happy. Do you think there is a difference in his happiness at each point?

Do you recognize anything of yourself in the stonemason?

A Different Chirp

by Nel de Theije-Avontuur

One fine day, a big green cricket sprung onto a grassy bank in the woods. It had traveled on a warm wind current from another country. For a few moments, the cricket sat and looked around him, getting his bearings after the long journey. Then he saw another cricket, a little cricket, sitting on another grassy bank nearby. He was curious and wanted to get to know this little creature.

The large and the small crickets looked at each other and both of them thought, "Maybe we can play together." Then the big cricket made a huge jump, landed near the little one, and in his own chirpy language said, "Hello. Would you like to play with me?"

The little cricket jumped in fright to see the big cricket so close by—and chirping in some strange way that he couldn't understand. "Go away!" he chirped, angry at being so shocked.

"Come on!" chirped the big cricket, "I came up to you all friendly and wanted to play with you, and you get all angry at me. That's not nice."

The little one still couldn't understand a word he said, but he could tell by the tone that the big cricket was now angry as well. They both grew more and more angry and soon they had started punching each other with their front legs.

Fortunately an old cricket came along. The old cricket had traveled to many different countries and could understand both of them. "Hey, this isn't fun; is it?" he said to the little cricket. "What would you rather be doing?"

"I wanted to play with him," the cricket responded.

"And what would you like to do?" the old cricket asked the big one.

"I just came over to ask if he wanted to play with me."

"Well," laughed the old cricket, "then I know what you're going to do. You both want the same thing. Play together!"

"This is for all of you," she said.

Four Words

by Erich Kaniok

In a busy market in a seaside town, four children from different countries were begging with outstretched hands. A woman came along and wanted to give each of the children something, but she had only one coin. "This is for all of you," she said. "Buy something to share."

One of the children said, "I'll go and buy us some angur."

"No," said one of the other children. "I'll buy us some inab."

"Oh, no you won't!" cried the third child. "I don't want angur, and I don't want inab. I want uzüm!"

"I don't want any of that stuff," grumbled the fourth child. "I want stafi!"

And it didn't stop at grumbling. Soon it became cursing and then hitting and punching. They just didn't stop. By chance, the woman saw the children again on her way home. This woman spoke many different languages, and she heard one of the children speaking Farsi, the next one speaking Arabic, the third using Turkish, and the fourth one speaking Greek. (Well, I say spoke, but actually they were yelling.)

The woman realized that the four little fighters hadn't even noticed that they had dropped the coin on the ground. She picked it up, walked off, and came back a little later. She stood in the midst of the children and said, "Did you know that each of you were saying you wanted the same thing—but in your own language? Grapes. I went to buy them for you. Here you are."

DISCUSSION

◉ **The Stories**

"A Different Chirp" is suitable for children ages 6–8.

"Four Words" is suitable for children ages 8–12.

Central Theme

Misunderstandings; language problems that lead to arguments.

Underlying Themes

The value of the insight and knowledge of others.

The role of a person who sees how a misunderstanding has come about and is able to help resolve it.

Developmental Concepts

Social-emotional development: Examining the development of conflicts and the possibilities for resolution.

Community, values, and norms: Reflecting on friendship: the causes, prevention, and resolution of arguments among friends. Preconceptions from lack of understanding, not comprehending other people.

Open Questions and Guidelines

For Children Ages 6–8, Relating to "A Different Chirp"

What exactly caused the argument between the crickets?

What would have happened if the older cricket hadn't come along?

Have you ever had an argument that was unnecessary? How did that come about? How was it resolved?

How do you make up after an argument? Has someone ever helped you to do that?

Do you think the older cricket was right? Do you think the big cricket and the little cricket will play together now?

For Children Ages 8–12, Relating to "Four Words"

What actually caused the argument between the children?

Why did it just keep getting worse?

What would have happened if the woman hadn't come back?

How can you tell another person something if you can't understand each other's languages?

Have you ever had an argument that wasn't necessary? How did that happen?

How might you make up after an argument?

Have you ever needed someone else to help you make up with a friend?

What do you think the children will do once they have the grapes?

The Three Kittens

by Nel de Theije-Avontuur

In the attic where they were born, three young kittens were playing. They usually played nicely with each other, but they also played roughly with each other from time to time.

Watching them playing together, the mama cat thought, "They are growing up quickly. It's about time they venture out and explore the world outside the attic. They will learn a lot."

So she called the three kittens to her and said, "Today you will be allowed to leave the attic for the first time to explore the world. And, as you explore, remember to leave signs of where you've traveled. When you return tonight, I will want to hear all about your experiences, and tomorrow we will go into the world together to see where you have been."

With that, the kittens left the attic together, but they soon separated, and each went his own way. As the first kitten ambled along, he thought, "I know what cats do to show everyone where they have been: They pee everywhere. It may not be able to be seen, but it can be smelled." So the kitten peed as much as he could, against every plant, wall, and tree he could find. And, because he wanted to pee so much, he had to drink a lot. He was a very busy kitten.

Strolling along, the second kitten suddenly heard a strange cat meowing. The cat was sitting above him in a tree. "I will make this neighborhood mine," the kitten thought, "but the other cat will need to get out of the tree first!" So he climbed into the tree until he came to the branch where the other cat was sitting. The kitten made himself really big, fluffed up his tail, and started hissing at the other cat. Frightened, the other cat jumped out of the tree.

"Well, I showed that cat who is boss!" thought the kitten.

The third kitten had a great day. He met lots of other cats, played with them, went mouse hunting with his new friends, and they all had a feast together. The other cats showed the kitten where they lived, and he in return told them about his mother and brothers.

When night came, all three kittens returned to the attic very tired.

"Before you three fall asleep," their mother said, "I want to hear what you have done today so I know you explored the great outside."

The first kitten said, "You can smell me everywhere. I peed everywhere I went!"

"And what about you?" the mother asked the second kitten.

"I made sure that every cat I met knew who was boss," he said. "You'll see that I scared them all away!"

"Now your turn," the mother cat said to the third kitten.

"I actually forgot that you wanted to hear about our experiences. But I met a lot of different cats, I went hunting with them, and I told them about us. I had a wonderful time."

"Very well. Now go to bed, the three of you," said the mother cat. "Tomorrow we will go outside and have a look to see where you have been."

It rained that night. When they went outside the next day, they could not find all the pee smells that the first kitten had left behind. The rain had washed clean the plants, walls, and trees. And in the neighborhood where the second kitten had traveled, they did not see any other cats at all. The second kitten had so frightened them that they hid as soon as they saw him coming. But they did meet the cats that the third kitten had visited. His new friends told the mama cat all about the wonderful time they had had.

That made the mother cat very proud and happy. "The other cats are glad you were there," she said to the third kitten. "You learned something important: Make friends. This is the best way to show others where you have been."

Signs on the Road

by Erich Kaniok

A father sent his two sons into the wide world. He thought it was about time they learned some life lessons so they could experience how people lived in the countryside, in a village, or in a town.

"Make sure you leave signs behind everywhere you go," he said to them both. "That way, I will know where you have been on your travels." And so the two brothers left their father and started on their journey.

After a couple of steps, the elder brother already started to leave signs. He stacked some stones on the roadside, made knots in tall grass, and broke some sticks off bushes and trees and stuck them in the ground. The entire path he walked was full of signs. He was so occupied with leaving signs that he hardly looked around him or met new people.

The younger brother began in a totally different way. He didn't make any signs at the side of the road. In the first village, he visited an inn, ate and drank with the local people, talked about his life, and listened to other people's stories about their way of life. In the next village, he befriended a boy who took him to meet his family where they lived in a small house in the countryside.

In a short time, this brother saw and experienced how life was in the countryside. Then he traveled farther and arrived in a town. Because he was a friendly and open-minded man, he soon met another family who offered him shelter. When they were having their dinner in the evening, he listened to their stories, their way of thinking, and how they dealt with certain situations. When it was his turn, he talked about his views of life.

In the meantime, the elder brother was really busy with his stones, knots, and sticks and getting really tired of bending over all the time to leave signs behind. When the two brothers returned home, they each explained their experiences to their father. He listened to their stories with his full attention and decided to travel along the same road as his sons had before him. Everywhere they went, the youngest son and his father were greeted with a lot of hospitality, but nobody knew the older son.

"I don't understand. Why does nobody know me?" he said. "Everybody is really friendly to my brother, and all he did was just look around and talk to people. He didn't stack a single stone, didn't put any knots in the tall grass, and didn't put any sticks in the ground. He didn't leave any signs behind as you requested, Father, but everybody knows him and likes him."

Then the father replied. "Signs can be made of more than just grass, sticks, and stones, my son. You also can leave behind signs on somebody else's heart when you meet them, talk to them, and make friends. Those are the signs that your brother left behind. That is why he is loved and recognized by the people. The signs left behind on people's hearts are forever. Grass, sticks, and stones will disappear one day.

DISCUSSION

◉ **The Stories**
"The Three Kittens" is suitable for children ages 6–8.
"Signs on the Road" is suitable for children ages 10–12.

◉ **Central Themes**
Finding your place in the world. Considering what kind of impression you leave on other people.

◉ **Underlying Themes**
Being involved. Being kind to people and being really interested in and learning from what other people have to say. Being honest about yourself.

◉ **Developmental Concepts**
Sharing feelings, wishes, and opinions. Taking other people into account and being open to others.

Considering friendship and the first impression you make when meeting new people. Respecting others and, especially, the differences in how people live, where they live, and what jobs they do.

◉ Open Questions and Guidelines

For Children Ages 6–8, Relating to "The Three Young Kittens"

How does the first kitten show where he has been? Why do you think he did that?

What did the second kitten do so others would remember him being there? Can you imagine why? Why did the third kitten forget what mother cat had asked him to do? Yet it was still possible to see where he had been. How did it show?

How do you think the story continues? What do you think the first kitten will do when he ventures out again? What about the second and third kittens? Explain your answer.

Have you ever visited somewhere where you had a nice time? How did you act?

How will other people remember you? How do you feel about that?

For Children Ages 10–12, Relating to "Signs on the Road"

What would you have done if you were one of the sons? Explain why.

The father was hoping that his sons would learn something on their travels. What do you think the eldest son learned? What do you think the youngest son learned?

What does the father mean when he talks about the "signs left behind on people's hearts"? What kind of signs have you left behind in your life so far? What do you think of those signs?

Imagine that you found happiness
by finding that nut.

The Lucky Nut

by Nel de Theije-Avontuur

"Do you know what I heard?" said one squirrel to the other.

"I have no idea," said the other. "What did you hear?"

"Well, in the tree where the owls were having their annual meeting, I heard an owl say that there is one very special nut. If you can find it, you will be happy."

"Oh, yes? And what else did he say about it?"

"He said that if you find that nut, you will know it right away because it is different. It feels warmer than all the other nuts."

"Did the owl say anything more about it?"

"Yes, he said that you have to take very good care of the nut. I didn't hear any more."

One of the squirrels quickly forgot the story, but the other one kept thinking about it. What if it were true? Imagine that you found happiness by finding that nut. You wouldn't have to worry about anything anymore, and you wouldn't need to do anything special to find happiness.

He made a plan: "I'm going to collect all the nuts in the woods—the beechnuts, the hazelnuts, the sweet chestnuts, and all the other nuts. I'll hold them for a moment to see if one feels warmer than the others, and then I'll throw them on a heap so that I'll know which ones I've already tried."

No sooner said than done. The squirrel picked up one nut after the other, held each for a moment, felt if one was warmer than another, and then threw them on a heap. He grabbed and felt, grabbed and felt. The pile of nuts that he had tried got higher and higher. The days passed by...many, many days passed by.

The squirrel thought of nothing else and did nothing except grab and feel. He forgot his friends. He forgot to eat. He forgot everything that was important to him. And then one day he forgot to feel. And on that very day, he picked up a nut that was warmer than all the others and…he just threw it on that huge pile of nuts.

The Touchstone

by Erich Kaniok

A man once found a story about a stone in a very old book. It was not just any old stone. It was a very special stone. Absolutely anything you touched with the stone would change into gold.

In the book, it said that the stone had come to rest on the beach by a huge lake. The beach, the book said, was full of stones and millions of pebbles. It also said that when you found the stone you would know it because the stone was strangely warmer than all the other stones. It would even make you feel warm.

After reading the story, the man could think of nothing but that one stone. So he went off in search of it. He sat on that beach and picked up one stone after another, let it sit in his hand for a moment to see if it was warm, and then threw it in the lake if it wasn't. That way he knew that he wouldn't pick up the same stone twice.

As he worked, he dreamed of everything he could do and everything he could have if he found that stone. In his mind, he saw everything turn to gold. How happy he would be! He picked up, felt, threw, picked up, felt, threw for days, for weeks, and for months. Bit by bit, he forgot about everything he had ever considered important—his wife, his children, his friends, his work…. He forgot everything that had ever made him happy. And then one day, he forgot to feel. He picked up a stone, a warm stone, held it in his hand and…threw it in the lake.

DISCUSSION

● **The Stories**

Little Man Finds a Home, by Max Velthuijs (see References), is a story with a similar theme for children ages 4–6.

"The Lucky Nut" is suitable for children ages 6–8.

"Touchstone" is suitable for ages 8–12.

● **Central Themes**

Happiness. Looking for happiness and forgetting to live. Considering happiness through questions such as:

Is happiness the same for everyone?

Can you find happiness by searching for it?

Can you "have" happiness in the sense of possessing it?

Can you make other people happy?

What is necessary in order to recognize happiness?

How can happiness escape you?

● **Underlying Theme**

Allowing ourselves to focus on one thing to the exclusion of all others in our lives makes it possible to forget what is really important.

● **Developmental Concepts**

Discovering yourself includes discovering what can make you happy. Sharing happiness with other people. Making someone happy.

● **Open Questions and Guidelines**

For Children Ages 6–8, Relating to "Lucky Nut"

What actually happens in this story? Why does the squirrel end up throwing away the only warm nut?

If the squirrel had not thrown away the lucky nut, would he have been happy? Why?

Will the squirrel who didn't go looking for the nut ever find happiness? What do you think?

What does happiness means to you?

For Children Ages 8–10, Relating to "Touchstone"

The man threw the warm stone into the lake. How did that happen?

Would he have been happy if he hadn't thrown that stone into the lake? What do you think? Why?

What is happiness for you? Something big? Something small? A moment? A memory? Can you tell us about something that makes you happy?

Can you find happiness by looking for it or does it take more than that? Can you make another person happy? How?

For Children Ages 10–12, Relating to "Touchstone"

The man throws away a warm stone. How did that happen?

What do you think would have happened if the man had realized that he had found the right stone? Would he have been happy? What do you think and why?

What is happiness for you? Something big? Something small? A moment? A memory? Can you tell us something about it?

Would you like to make someone else happy? Who? How?

Can you find happiness by looking for it, or does it take more than that?

Is happiness different for everyone? What do you think? Why?

What do you think is meant by a stone that can turn everything into gold?

The Young Bird of Prey

by Nel de Theije-Avontuur

In a nest high in a tree, a young bird of prey was born. His father and mother nourished him. They would hunt and catch mice, birds, young rabbits, and other animals. They carried their catches back to the nest and gave the young bird the best pieces of meat.

Soon the young bird of prey was growing up and was big enough to start hunting for himself. Mother and father taught him how to hunt by dropping a piece of meat in the air that he had to catch. They dropped a piece of meat from a branch they were sitting on, and the young bird had to try to catch it before it fell to the ground. He did well.

"And now for your final lesson," said the father bird.

"Come with us," said the mother bird. With the warm wind beneath their wings, they climbed higher and higher, circling in the air until the father thought they were high enough.

"Pay attention to father," said the mother.

The father climbed a bit higher in the sky, spread his wings out fully, and hovered motionless in the sky.

"What is he doing that for?" asked the young bird.

"He's looking for prey," said the mother.

"Where?" asked the young bird. "I don't see anything on the ground."

"That's because you are not keeping still."

All of a sudden, the father dropped to the ground like a stone, grabbed something with his claws, and flew up to a branch. The young bird of prey joined his father on the branch and was offered a piece of the mouse that the older bird had captured.

"Now you try," said his father.

After a lot of practice, the young bird finally managed to hover in the air without flapping his wings. And then he realized that he could see everything on the ground very clearly. He spotted something tasty—a big fat locust. He let himself drop, just as he had seen his father do...and, yes, he caught the locust.

"Now eat him," said his father and mother. "And listen while you eat because now you will learn your final lesson. We birds of prey hunt and catch prey to eat and to feed our young. We do not hunt for any other reason because if you kill for no reason bad things will happen. Do you understand?"

"I understand," said the young bird.

"Do you promise?"

"Yes, yes, I do," answered the young bird, and he kept his promise...at least for the first day. But on the second day he thought, "I can catch a lot more." So he kept hunting and hunting until he couldn't eat any more, and he left all the dead animals on a branch or on the ground. On the third day, he was enjoying hunting so much that he couldn't stop himself. Floating high, keeping dead still, plunging to catch his prey, killing and leaving the dead animal behind. And again: Floating high, keeping dead still, dropping on his prey, killing and leaving the dead animal behind. And again. He hung dead still in the air...saw a mouse...and thought, "I'm going to catch you!" and... he missed! He ended up with his beak stuck in the ground!

You might have thought that birds couldn't get headaches. But this one sure did!

Invisible Hunters

(Adapted by Nel de Theije-Avontuur from
De koning en de Indiaan: Verhalen uit Nicaragua
[The king and the Indian: Stories from Nicaragua] by Dick Bloemraad,
Susan Breedijk, Fiona Macintosh, and Landelijk Stedenbanden
Nederland-Nicaragua)

[NOTE: *This is a story of the Miskito Indians, a group of original inhabitants of Nicaragua in Central America.*]

One evening, three young brothers from the village Ulwas, on the river Rio Coco, were hunting. They were looking for "waris," a kind of wild boar.

After walking in the jungle for an hour, they heard a noise: "Dar…dar…dar…" The brothers stood still and looked around but didn't see a thing. Then they heard the noise again. It came out of a tree covered with vines. One brother grabbed one of the vines and suddenly disappeared into thin air. Another brother grabbed one of the vines, and he, too, disappeared. The third brother let out a worried yell: "What have you done to my brothers?"

"I haven't done anything to your brothers," a voice replied. "When they let go of my vines, you will see them again." The two brothers let go of the vines they were holding on to and reappeared.

"Who are you?" the brothers asked surprised.

"I am the Dar," said the voice. "When somebody grabs me, he will become invisible to man and animal."

The brothers looked at each other in wonder. That would come in handy to catch waris, each was thinking! The three brothers held their hands out to grab a vine.

"Wait, wait!" the Dar screamed out. "You can't just do that. Before you take something that belongs to me, you have to promise that you will use my powers for doing good."

"We promise you. Whatever you want," said the brothers.

"Well, listen to what I have to say," the Dar said. "You must promise that you will not sell the meat of the waris. You are allowed only to give it away."

That was not a problem for the brothers, as they always shared their meat with the rest of the village.

"Furthermore," said the Dar, "you can hunt using only the traditional Indian way. You have to catch and kill the waris as quickly as possible. The animal should not suffer."

This was another easy request for the brothers.

"And you are not allowed to use guns," the Dar finished. That was really easy too as the brothers did not own any guns.

That day, the brothers caught a lot of waris with the help of the Dar's vines, which made them invisible. When they had enough, the brothers returned the vine to the Dar and headed home. In the village, they shared the meat with their neighbors. Of course people had a lot of questions, and the brothers told their story of meeting the Dar.

The elders of the village knew the power of the Dar. "The Dar is very old and very powerful," they said. "As long as you keep your promise to the Dar, everybody will be rewarded."

Time passed, and everybody was happy until one day when two merchants arrived by boat. The merchants heard stories about the extraordinary hunters and wanted to buy some wari meat. The brothers reminded themselves about their promise to share the meat. But to this one brother added, "But when all the villagers have had their share, we might have some meat left that we can sell."

"But the Dar will find out!" said another of the brothers.

In the end, they decided to sell the meat anyway. All was well until one day when the merchants demanded more meat and even wanted the villagers' share of the catch. "Your way of hunting is too slow," the merchants also told the hunters. "You can use our guns so you can catch more waris."

The brothers did not like that idea at all until one of them said, "Maybe the merchants are a lot more powerful than the Dar." The thought made the brothers forget their promise to the Dar and forget to take care of their village. Soon they were getting richer and richer—but they had broken all of their promises to the Dar.

And then one day, about the time the brothers should have been returning from their hunt, the villagers looked up and could not believe their eyes. Instead of hunters, all they saw was a strange and slow procession of dead waris.

[A NOTE TO THE LEADER: It might be a good idea to stop the story here. The children will have the opportunity to voice their ideas of what happened to the hunters and how the story will continue. If you choose not to end here, the original story continues as follows.]

That day, after the hunt, although the brothers had returned the vines to the Dar, they did not become visible again. It did not matter how much they begged and pleaded; the Dar did not answer them and only repeated: "Dar... dar...dar..."

So, not knowing what else to do, the brothers returned to the village in their invisible form. Seeing the strange sight of the dead waris, the elders understood what had happened. "You can't live here anymore," they said to the brothers. "You all need to leave Ulwas."

To this day, some of the Miskito Indians believe that the hunters still wander the banks of the Rio Coco, forever pleading with the Dar to make them visible again. Some even claim that invisible hunters walked next to them in the forest. They said they are sure because they heard voices calling out: "Dar...dar...dar..."

DISCUSSION

⊙ **The Stories**

Elephant and Crocodile, by Max Velthuijs and Anthea Bell (see References), is a story with a similar theme suitable for children ages 4–6.

"The Young Bird of Prey" is suitable for children ages 6–8.

"Invisible Hunters" is suitable for children ages 8–12.

⊙ **Central Theme**

Betraying trust and being tempted by wealth.

⊙ **Underlying Themes**

Forgetting promises. Hunting for food vs. hunting for profit, hunting and unnecessary killing.

⊙ **Developmental Concepts**

Making choices, keeping promises, resisting temptation.

Learning to see differences. Separating one's own interests from group interests. Preserving nature.

⊙ **Open Questions and Guidelines**

For Children Ages 6–8, Relating to "The Young Bird of Prey"
The parents of the young bird are trying to teach him something about hunting. What do you think was the most important lesson?

They explained the reason why they hunt. Do you think the young bird misunderstood his parents or was something else on his mind? If so, what do you think that was?

Can you explain the different ways of hunting? Explain how the parents taught their young bird and explain how the young bird experienced hunting.

"...he missed...and ended up with his beak stuck in the ground!" What's your opinion about that?

Are you good at keeping the promises you make? Why or why not?

For Children Ages 8–10, Relating to "Invisible Hunters"
If you decide to stop the story at the point of the procession of dead waris, give the children the opportunity to explain in their own words what they think happened and how the story will continue. Make sure they explain why their ending makes sense.

The Dar makes the brothers promise that they will share the meat, kill the waris in the traditional Indian way, and not hunt using guns. Why do you think the Dar made the brothers promise that? Why did it become more and more difficult to keep that promise?

Are you good at keeping the promises you make? Why or why not?

The elders banish the three brothers from the village. Do you understand the reason for this? Do you agree with the elders? Why or why not?

For Children Ages 10–12, Relating to "Invisible Hunters"

If you decide to stop the story at the point of the dead waris procession, give the children the opportunity to explain in their own words what they think happened and how the story will continue. Make sure they explain why their ending makes sense.

"Maybe the merchants are a lot more powerful than the Dar," suggested one of the brothers. Do you think that the brothers believe this is true even as they say it?

Do you think it is important that your friends, relatives, and other people keep their promises? Do you think it is important to keep your own promises?

This is an ancient story that is still being told in Nicaragua. Do you know why?

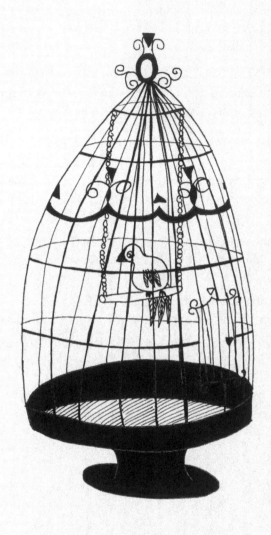

Its cage was of pure gold
and the finest silver.

The Bird

by Erich Kaniok and Leo Kaniok

One day the people in a far-off land saw a beautiful bird. The feathers on his head and chest were a deep blue; those on his wings shone bright red. He sung like a nightingale, flew like a bird of paradise, and had beautiful eyes like a hummingbird. Everyone could see that this bird was a very special bird.

The king saw it, too, and wanted to have the wild bird for his own. He gave his men orders to capture the bird. "But take care," warned the king. "I don't want anything to happen to it!"

One night, one of the king's men crept into the tree where the bird slept and caught it. The king was very happy and treated the captured bird in the same way he would wish to be treated himself. He gave the bird everything he could think of. Its cage was of pure gold and the finest silver. Musicians played music to the bird, dancers danced for him, poets read poems to him, and storytellers told him stories.

The king had the most delicious food prepared for him: roast chicken, delicious rice, and fragrant tea. But the bird didn't eat. He didn't look at the dancers. He didn't listen to the poets and storytellers. He didn't want to hear any music. His deep blue feathers became dull. His bright red wings lost their bloom. He couldn't fly like a bird of paradise in his little cage, and he no longer had the will to sing like a nightingale. His eyes looked like the eyes of a sick sparrow. After three days, the bird died.

The king was inconsolable; he could not understand why the bird had died.

"I treated him just as I myself would wish to have been treated. I gave him everything I would have wanted myself," he thought. "Why was that not good enough for this bird?"

- **The Story**

  The Little Boy and the Big Fish, by Max Velthuijs (see References), is a story with a similar theme for children ages 4–6.

  "The Bird" is suitable for ages 6–12.

- **Central Themes**

  Freedom. Second-guessing what someone else wants, however good your intentions, can keep the other person prisoner. What you like is not necessarily what another person enjoys.

- **Underlying Themes**

  Finding the freedom to be yourself.

  Respecting the differences between living beings and what keeps them alive.

- **Developmental Concepts**

  Learning to care for the physical and mental health of oneself and others.

  Community, norms, and values: Understanding that one's ideas about life are not necessarily shared by others. Getting along with other cultures and other life forms.

- **Open Questions and Guidelines**

  For Children Ages 6–8

  The king said, "I gave him everything I would have wanted myself. Why was that not good enough for this bird?" Do you know why?

  Why do you think the king wanted to own the bird?

  Have you ever really, really wanted something? What was it? Why did you want it?

  Why did the bird not enjoy being in the cage? Have you ever felt that way? How did that feel? Did your situation come out all right in the end?

  For Children Ages 8–10

  Begin with the questions that were used with children ages 6–8 and then add these:

  The king gave the bird the things he liked himself. Who was he thinking about most: himself or the bird? What do you think about that?

  What did the bird want?

For Children Ages 10–12

Why did the king want the bird?

Why didn't the bird like being in the cage? Have you ever felt that way? What was that like? How did you solve your situation?

The king gave the bird what he himself liked. Who was he thinking about most? What do you think about that? What did the bird want?

The king said to himself, "I treated [the bird] just as I myself would wish to have been treated. Why was that not good enough for this bird?" Had the roles been reversed, do you think it would have been enough for the king?

Have you ever had a situation where someone else decided what you should enjoy? How was that?

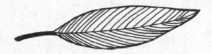

"Would you like to be my pet?"
Jesse asked the bug.

Jesse's Pet

by Nel de Theije-Avontuur

At Jesse's house, they didn't have any pets: no dog, no cat, no rabbit, no chickens. It was not because Jesse didn't want pets, but it just wasn't possible for the family to have one.

"Can we really not have a pet?" Jesse would ask his parents over and over.

"No, absolutely not," was always the answer.

So instead, Jesse talked to and played with any animal that he came upon, from a bird to a hedgehog to the smallest bug. One day, Jesse came upon an interesting bug—a big cricket! Jesse's held out his hand, and the bug crawled on it. The bug's tiny feet tickled, but Jesse didn't mind.

"Would you like to be my pet?" Jesse asked the bug. He thought he saw the bug nod "Yes" with its head.

So Jesse popped the bug in a box, took it inside, and hid it under his bed. The bug stayed there all night and all the next day while Jesse was at school. When he got home, he ran to the bedroom to see the bug. He was shocked to find that the bug didn't look well at all. It was barely moving and its antennae, which yesterday had stood up straight, were drooping.

"Don't you want to live in this box?" asked Jesse. "Maybe you don't want to be a pet."

When the bug did nothing, Jesse sighed. "I'll take you back outside."

Outside, Jesse opened the box again. "Come on out," he coaxed. The bug didn't move. "You don't have to stay in the box any more. I know you're not a pet." Now the bug walked around the box in a circle, but it didn't come out.

"Why don't you come out of the box? Do you think that you can't? Have you forgotten that you can fly?" asked Jesse. "Shall I get you out?"

The bug didn't say "No." So Jesse stuck his finger in the box. The bug climbed onto his finger. "You're such a lovely bug. You crickets can jump really well. And now you're free. Free to jump wherever you want to. Off you hop!"

[NOTE TO THE LEADER: *To open a discussion with the children here, the story could end here with the question: What do you think happened next? Why? If you choose not to end the story here, it continues below.*]

And then the bug hopped off into the bushes!

You have the heart of an eagle.
You are an eagle.

The Displaced Eagle

by Erich Kaniok

High in the mountains, a man found a young eagle sitting by an abandoned nest. The man waited at a safe distance to see if the adult eagles would come back with food for the young one. But they did not come—not that day nor the following day. By then the eaglet had become weak from hunger, and the man decided to take it home with him. He put the eaglet with his chickens and gave it chicken feed to eat.

Five years later, a biologist came to visit the man. As the two men were walking around the garden, they passed the chicken run. With a start, the biologist said, "That bird! That's an eagle, not a chicken!"

"That's right," said the man, "but he's grown up with the chickens. He's become a chicken now, instead of an eagle."

"An eagle will always be an eagle," said the biologist. "Let me show you." He perched the eagle on his arm and raised it high, saying, "Spread your wings and fly!"

But the eagle saw the chickens pecking at their food, so he jumped from the man's arm, landed on the ground, and began foraging.

The man said, "I told you so. He has become a chicken."

"No," said the biologist. "It is an eagle, and I will prove it to you."

The next morning, he took the eagle to the roof of the house and said, "You are an eagle. You should be flying high in the sky. Stretch out your wings and fly!" But again the eagle jumped down when he saw the chickens pecking at the grain, and he joined them eating.

The man said, "I'll say it one more time. He is a chicken."

"No," insisted the biologist. "He is an eagle, and he still has the heart of an eagle. Give him one more chance."

The next morning, he took the eagle into the mountains. He lifted him up and said, "You have the wings of an eagle, and you have the heart of an eagle. You are an eagle. You can fly high in the air. You are free. Stretch out your wings and fly! Fly in the way only a powerful eagle can fly. Fly!"

[NOTE TO THE LEADER: To open a discussion with the children here, you could end the story with a question: What do you think happened next? Why? If you choose not to end the story here, it continues below.]

And then the eagle spread his huge wings, flew up with a screech, circled higher and higher in the air, and did not return.

DISCUSSION

◉ **The Stories**

"Jesse's Pet" is suitable for children ages 6–8.

"The Displaced Eagle" is suitable for children ages 8–12.

◉ **Central Theme**

Limiting the freedom of another by deciding who or how he should be.

◉ **Underlying Themes**

Becoming who you are supposed to be in spite the circumstances that might stand in your way.

Finding the strength to be yourself through someone who believes in you.

◉ **Developmental Concepts**

Becoming or being who you are. Allowing another person to be who he/she is; respecting another person's self-image. Wanting and daring to accept help.

Dealing with times when you do not know who you are or what you want.

◉ **Open Questions and Guidelines**

For Children Ages 6–8, Relating to "Jesse's Pet"

Did the cricket want to be a pet? What do you think? Why?

Jesse thought the bug wanted to be his pet. How do you think that happened?

Why were the bug's antennae drooping? How do you think the bug was feeling? Have you ever felt that way?

Why did the cricket refuse to come out of the box at first? In the end, what made him come out?

Have you ever thought you couldn't do something anymore? Can you do it now? What helped you to do it again?

For Children Ages 8–10, Relating to "The Displaced Eagle"

Should the man have put the eagle in the chicken coop or not? What do you think? What else could he have done?

Was he right when he said the eagle had become a chicken?

Have you ever felt like an eagle in a cage? Did that feeling pass? What helped?

At first, the eagle hesitated to fly. Why? What happened when he later flew?

For Children Ages 10–12, Relating to "The Displaced Eagle"

What do you think about the man putting the eagle in the chicken coop? Could he have done something else?

Did the eagle become a chicken in that coop? Do you think he felt like a chicken, or do you think he felt like an eagle that had to behave like a chicken?

Have you ever felt like an eagle in a chicken coop? How was that for you?

Can you imagine that some people feel like an eagle in a chicken coop? How might that happen? Can that be changed? How?

At first, the eagle refused to fly away. Why? Why did it later fly away?

Do you think it helped that the biologist believed that he could behave like an eagle again? Has it ever helped you when someone believed that you could do something or be something?

The Horse's Three Questions

by Nel de Theije-Avontuur

Horse was the leader of a large herd of horses who lived on a huge grassy prairie. They had plenty of grass to eat and enough water to drink. There was nothing more they could wish for...and yet...Horse felt that something was missing.

When he thought about it, Horse realized that he wanted to understand the purpose of his life. He wanted to know that his existence was important and had meaning.

"What should I do? With whom? When?" Horse often found himself wondering.

He took his questions to the older horses. He then asked the mares with their foals. But none of the other horses' answers satisfied him.

One day, deep in thought, Horse wandered off from the herd until he was all alone. Suddenly, he saw a very old horse in the distance. As he galloped over, he saw that the old horse was not alone. A very young foal lay on the ground nearby, looking very tired, hungry, and thirsty—no doubt the foal was lost.

"Hello, horse," Horse called to the old horse. "You are so old. You must have an answer to the three most important questions in my life: What should I do? With whom? When?"

"Shall we first help this little one?" asked the old horse.

"Yes, of course," said Horse. He bent down, spoke some encouraging words to the foal, and, with the old horse's help, got the little one back on his feet. Horse led the foal back to the herd and to his mother. Immediately the foal perked up and began to take milk from her. When all was settled, Horse returned to the old horse.

"Now will you answer my questions?" he asked.

"You have answered the questions yourself," said the old horse. "What should you do? Whatever is needed. That foal needed your help. With whom? With whoever is there. When? At the moment that you can do something."

Horse was quiet for a moment. And then, with a whinny, he bowed his head to the old horse and trotted back to the herd.

Three Life Questions

by Erich Kaniok

Long ago in Russia, there lived a tsar who had everything a person could wish for. But the tsar was restless. He did not know what his purpose in life was. Three questions about his life's purpose nagged at him: "What should I do? With whom? When?"

In vain, he consulted all the wise men and women in the kingdom. No one could help him. And then one day, he heard about a farmer, far away, who might be able to give him an answer. Without delay, the tsar went in search of the farmer, and, after several weeks, he reached the country—and the farm—where the man lived. The farmer barely looked up as the tsar asked his questions. He didn't answer when the tsar had finished. Calmly, he just continued plowing his field.

The tsar grew quite angry. "Do you know who I am?" he asked the farmer. "I am tsar of all Russia." But even this statement made no impression on the farmer who continued with his work.

Suddenly, out of the forest, limped a badly wounded man. The stranger fell right in front of the farmer's plow.

"Will you help me carry this man to my hut?" the farmer asked, speaking to the tsar at last.

"I will help you, but will you then answer my questions?" responded the tsar.

"Later," said the farmer, and together they took the man to the hut and bandaged his wounds.

"Now will you answer my questions?" asked the tsar when they had finished.

"You can go home now," the farmer answered. "You have answered the questions yourself. What should you do? Whatever comes your way. With whom should you do it? With whoever is there. You helped me with this wounded man. When should you do it? At the right moment."

DISCUSSION

◉ **The Stories**

"The Horse's Three Questions" is suitable for children ages 6–10.

"Three Life Questions" is suitable for children ages 10–12.

◉ **Central Themes**

Do what you can do.

Finding meaning and purpose in life. Recognizing what is asked of you.

Self-knowledge. Valuing yourself. Knowing what you can do, doing something with that, and being proud of it.

Taking responsibility. Sometimes taking responsibility for someone else.

◉ **Underlying Themes**

Doubting the purpose of life. Every moment can be fulfilling when you do what needs to be done.

Care. The helpless foal and the wounded man needed care.

Respect for the insights and wisdom of another.

◉ **Developmental Concepts**

Being unique. Knowing and respecting your own capabilities and your own limitations. Taking care of yourself and of others.

Expressing your feelings. Dealing with doubt.

Learning to respect and care for others.

◉ Open Questions and Guidelines

For Children Ages 6–8, Relating to "The Horse's Three Questions"

What was Horse actually missing?

After the two horses helped the foal, the old horse said to Horse, "You have answered the questions yourself." What did he mean by that?

Are you sometimes unsure about what you should do? When has this happened? Why?

At these times, could the old horse's answer help you, too?

For Children Ages 8–10, Relating to "The Horse's Three Questions"

What was bothering Horse? How did he find the answers?

What did Horse and the old horse do for the foal? Why?

What did the old horse mean by, "You have answered the questions yourself"? Do you think that Horse now knows what is important in his life?

Are you sometimes unsure about what you should do? At these times, could the old horse's answer help you, too?

For Children Ages 10–12, Relating to "Three Life Questions"

What was bothering the tsar?

Can you answer the tsar's questions in your own words? Ask those questions of yourself: What should I do? With whom? When?

Have you ever thought, "I'll do that some time but not now"? Do you now think, "I wish I had done it when I could"?

Why did the farmer not answer the tsar immediately? Why did he answer later?

What did the wounded man need? Did he get what he needed from the tsar and the farmer?

The story does not say how the tsar reacted to the farmer's answer. How do you think he reacted?

"Grandfather, I think we
should build the new anthill
a bit farther into the forest."

Grandfather Ant and Little Ant

by Nel de Theije-Avontuur

Somewhere down the forest path, Grandfather Ant was having a stroll. In front of him, his grandson Little Ant was darting from left to right, sometimes shooting forward and then back. He had to smell this, touch that, and even dig a little here and there.

Little Ant, his grandfather, grandmother and all the members of the Ant family lived in an anthill nearby. It had become too small for them all. So somebody had to find a good place for a new anthill. And that somebody was Grandfather Ant. He was the oldest of them all, he had lived the longest of them all, and he knew all the best locations. Little Ant, a very young ant, wanted to help. And this is how it happened that they were both walking through the forest.

"Grandfather, this is a good spot," Little Ant cried suddenly. "I can smell it, I can feel it, and you can easily dig here!"

Grandfather replied: "Isn't this a bit too close to the forest path, Little Ant?"

"No," said Little Ant. "This is a very good spot. And you can easily drag all of our belongings here along the forest path." And that's how he started. He dug a hole. Then he began dragging sand, leaves, branches with pine needles, and all that the ants needed to make an anthill to the chosen spot. Grandfather was resting after the long walk. All of a sudden, the earth began to tremble underneath their feet. Grandfather and Little Ant heard "Step… step…step…"

Suddenly something huge appeared above them. It had very big feet and heavy shoes. A human! And that human put his feet right in the middle of the new anthill! Little Ant was trembling with fear. Then he became angry. He stomped and yelled and shouted! But a human can't hear an ant shout, so he just kept on walking.

"I will start again, Grandfather!" said Little Ant. He started to dig the same hole again and dragged all kinds of things into it.

"More humans might come," Grandfather warned.

"No way," said Little Ant, "I don't think so; this is a good spot. Did you see how easily I can drag all kinds of things to this place?"

"Yes, I can see that," said Grandfather. "But…"

Little Ant didn't listen to him and kept on working very hard. He was working so hard that he almost didn't notice that more humans were approaching. Grandfather managed to pull him away at the last second just before he got trampled by children's feet.

It is a fact that ants can't turn white because of fear, otherwise Little Ant would have been a white ant. He wanted to go and complain to the child, but he realized that the child might not even have noticed the anthill. He pondered this for a while then said, "Grandfather, I think we should build the new anthill a bit farther into the forest."

"That's a good idea, Little Ant," said grandfather, and together they started a new anthill for the whole Ant family.

The Gardener

by Erich Kaniok

A man had hired a gardener to care for his vegetable garden and flower beds. All of his gardens sat on a tiny, fenced piece of his property, not far from a small but strong-flowing stream.

The gardener studied the gardens. He told the owner, "If the stream outside the fence rises and threatens to flood the vegetable garden and the flower beds, I will try to hold the water back. But don't expect me to do anything outside the garden."

The owner said nothing.

Three springs came and went. Each spring, the stream swelled with water, burst its banks, and eventually flowed across the land and through the garden. Each year, the water destroyed everything in its path.

And now it was spring again. The sweat poured from the gardener as he tried to heap sand along the fence to keep the water out. But it was useless. No matter what he tried, the water continued to flow in from every side. Once again the gardens' seeds, plants, and flowers were all washed away.

The gardener sighed. Then he picked up a pickaxe and a shovel and walked toward the garden gate.

"Where are you off to?" called the owner who, until now, had paid no attention to what the gardener did. "You said you weren't going to work outside the garden."

"Yes, that's true," answered the gardener. "But now I'm going into the field outside the garden. No matter what I do in the garden and no matter how many sandbanks I make, I can't hold the water back. But if I go to the source, to where the stream is, I can make a dam and prevent the flooding."

The owner smiled.

DISCUSSION

◉ **The Stories**

"Grandfather Ant and Little Ant" is suitable for children ages 6–10.

"The Gardener" is suitable for children ages 10–12.

◉ **Central Theme**

Learning from your mistakes and taking responsibility for your own actions.

◉ **Underlying Themes**

The easiest way is not always the best way. Rigid thinking will stand in the way of finding solutions to a problem.

◉ **Developmental Concept**

Taking care of yourself and others. Acting in only your own interest is not the same as taking care of yourself.

Daring to learn from your own mistakes. Stubbornness can stand in the way of choosing and finding better solutions to a problem.

Community, norms, and values: Wanting to help others. Having the courage to change your opinion. Being responsible for completing a task.

● Open Questions and Guidelines

For Children Ages 6–8, Relating to "Grandfather Ant and Little Ant"

Why were Grandfather Ant and Little Ant trying to find a good location for a new anthill?

Why did Little Ant want to build a new anthill so close to the forest path? Grandfather didn't fully explain why he thought it was a bad idea. Why not?

Did Grandfather Ant tell Little Ant to build the anthill farther down the path? What did Little Ant learn?

Have you ever learned from your mistakes before? How did you feel about that?

For Children Ages 8–10, Relating to "Grandfather Ant and Little Ant"

What did the ants have to be aware of to be able to find a location for the new anthill?

Grandfather said: "Isn't this a bit too close to the forest path, Little Ant?" Why did he ask that?

Later, Little Ant said: "I think we should build the anthill farther into the forest." Why? What do you think Little Ant learned?

Have you ever had the experience of doing something the hard way before you realized there was an easier way? How did you react to that?

For Children Ages 10–12, Relating to "The Gardener"

The gardener worked for the owner of the garden. Why didn't he want to do work outside of the garden's boundaries? Do you think that was the right thing to do? Would it be nice to work like that?

The owner didn't say: "Told you so!" but smiled instead. Why do you think he just smiled?

Have you ever discovered that you were doing something the hard way before you realized there was an easier way? What did you do? What did you experience? How did you feel about that afterward?

The Five French Fries

by Nel de Theije-Avontuur

In the middle of town, there was a stand selling french fries. It was called the Five French Fries. Sam cooked up the best french fries in the world at this stand—at least, that's what he thought. And the people who came to taste them agreed. The trouble was, hardly any people came. In order to get more customers, Sam put a painted signboard on the pavement with a bag of—yes, five french fries. But that didn't help much.

"What can I do to get more customers?" sighed Sam.

"No idea," said the customer who had just bought a bag of Sam's fries.

At that moment, another customer came along. "Is business not going very well?" he asked.

"Not really," said Sam "Do you have any ideas?"

"Sure I have! Do you know what you should do?" the customer asked. "Change that signboard. Leave most of it the same, only instead of five, paint four french fries in the bag."

"What kind of nonsense is that?" asked Sam.

"Believe me! I'm certain it will work!" the customer replied.

[NOTE TO THE LEADER: *You might want to ask the children, "What do you think of this idea? Could it work? Why or why not?" And then the story continues below.*]

Since Sam didn't have any better ideas, he decided to try out what the customer had suggested. He set the new signboard on the pavement. "I'm curious to see what will happen," he said.

And this is what happened: Someone walked by, looked at the board, looked again, and then went up to Sam and said, "What you've got on that board is wrong. If you call your stand the Five French Fries, then you should show five fries in the picture—not four! And since I'm here, let me taste those fries of yours."

A little while later, the same thing happened—and it happened over and over again, all day long. That customer's idea had worked like a dream! Lots of people tried the french fries and came back for more. And Sam? He was happy of course, although he often wondered why that strange idea worked so well. But every year when he repainted his sign, he made sure it showed four—not five—french fries.

DISCUSSION

◉ **The Story**

Rosie and Roger, by Rik Dessers (see References), is a story with a similar theme for children ages 4–6.

"The Five French Fries" is suitable for children ages 6–12.

◉ **Central Theme**

Dealing with your faults and the faults of other people.

◉ **Underlying Theme**

Advertising makes use of human tendencies. In this case, it is the human tendency to point out other people's mistakes. Sometimes you need courage to show another person where something is really not good or wrong.

◉ **Developmental Concepts**

Social-emotional development: Dealing with your own faults and those of others.

Consumer behavior: Awareness of the effects of advertising.

Community, norms, and values: Seeing something wrong and dealing with it.

◉ **Open Questions and Guidelines**

The question posed in the middle of the story gives the children the space to consider their own thoughts about whether the idea will work or not and why.

◉ **Questions at the End of the Story:**

For Children Ages 6–8

The new customer's idea worked, and more people came to try the french fries. Can you explain why that idea worked?

Would you have told Sam that his sign showing the four french fries didn't make sense? Why? Why not?

What do you do most often—tell someone that she has done something right or tell her that she's done something wrong? What would you prefer to hear yourself? Why?

For Children Ages 8–10

The new customers come because of the sign. Why does the new sign work?

Pointing out each other's faults is human. How do you deal with other people's faults? Why?

How do you deal with the things that other people do well?

How do you feel when people point out your faults? Why?

Have you ever been in a situation where someone said or did something that really wasn't right? What was it? How did you react? Why?

For Children Ages 10–12

The new customers come because of the sign. Why does the new sign work?

That sign makes use of knowledge and understanding about how people react. How does that apply in this instance?

Can you think of a particular advertisement you have seen or heard in which the advertisers make use of knowledge and understanding about how people function?

Pointing out each other's faults is human. How do you deal with other people's faults? Why?

How do you deal with the things other people do well?

How do you feel when people point out your faults? Why?

Have you ever been in a situation where someone said or did something that really wasn't good? What was it? How did you react? Why?

Once there were two families who
lived underground:
the Mouse family and the Mole family.

The Mole and the Mouse

by Nel de Theije-Avontuur

Once there were two families who lived underground: the Mouse family and the Mole family. Both families had just had babies, and, of course, they were very hungry all of the time. All the parents were kept very busy just feeding them. Mama and Papa Mole were scrambling through the underground passages looking for worms, snails, and other tasty snacks. Mama and Papa Mouse were looking for food above ground to feed their babies: seeds of the fields, breadcrumbs, cake, and bits of cheese that they found in the house where the humans lived.

One day Papa Mole and Papa Mouse bumped into each other in one of the underground passages. Papa Mouse talked about the fields full of seeds and flowers and about all the little animals who lived there.

"Mmmm…" thought Papa Mole, "tasty treats!"

Papa Mouse also spoke about the house and about the humans, the dog that he liked, and the scary cat who lived there.

When Papa Mole returned home, he told his wife and children about the other world above ground. "I think I'll go and investigate," he said.

No sooner said than done, Papa Mole went out the next morning to investigate this new world. He walked all the way to the end of the passage and started to dig right above his head. Suddenly, it all went very bright, and Papa Mole was sitting on a huge molehill. And what did he see? Absolutely nothing! His eyes were blinded by the bright sunlight.

Papa Mole quickly crawled back underground and shuffled back into his hole. "There is nothing above the ground!" he said to his wife and the babies. "All I saw was lots of bright light. Papa Mouse made it all up."

"Listen to your father," said Mama Mole, "because Papa knows best!"

The Wise Hen

by Erich Kaniok and Leo Kaniok

The swifts were huddled together on the electricity wires around the farm. They were twittering, telling each other their stories, but their thoughts turned toward the end of the summer. Autumn was coming, and the northern winds were just around the corner. The time was approaching for their trip to the south. And one day, all of a sudden, they were all gone.

The hens heard the swifts twittering about their trip. "I think I'll also travel to the south next year," said one of them. The winter passed. The swifts returned, built their nests, and had their young. And when the northern winds arrived, they huddled together on the wires again, ready to leave.

The hens did not pay attention to the swifts this year. They were busy talking about the trip the hen was planning to take. One early morning, when the wind blew from the north, all the swifts left. They felt the wind underneath their wings, and they trusted their age-old instincts to guide them on their travels to the south, over the sea, to Africa.

"I think the wind is blowing from the right direction," the hen said that same morning. She spread her wings and ran out of the hen house as fast as she could. Flapping her wings wildly, she ran down the road until she reached a garden. When the evening arrived, she returned to the hen house, panting heavily. She told her story of how she traveled all the way to the south, all the way to the road where she saw the traffic of the big world pass her by. She traveled to countries where potatoes grew, and she had seen people working in fields. At the end of the road, she had found a garden with roses, the most beautiful roses. The gardener was there, too.

"How very interesting," the other hens said, "and how beautifully you describe your journey!"

Another winter passed. Springtime arrived and so did the swifts. They were talking about their trip, about flying over a sea. But the hens cluck-clucked when the swifts mentioned flying over a sea. "That's not what our hen said," they argued, "and she knows everything about traveling to the south."

DISCUSSION

● **The Stories**

"The Mole and the Mouse" is suitable for children ages 6–8.

"The Wise Hen" is suitable for children ages 8–12.

● **Central Theme**

The world is different for everyone. Go past the boundaries of your own world.

● **Underlying Theme**

Always wanting to be right can keep you from learning the truth.

● **Developmental Concepts**

Discovering what is important for yourself but being open to what is important to others.

Learning that our multicultural society has a multitude of internal worlds including your own. Getting to know each other's internal worlds can be an enriching experience.

● **Open Questions and Guidelines**

For Children in Ages 6–8, Relating to "The Mole and the Mouse"
Who was right? Papa Mouse or Papa Mole? Explain why.

When Papa Mole reported what he had seen above ground, Mama Mole said, "Listen to your father because Papa knows best!" Is she right? What do you think?

Papa Mole could have said something about his experiences other than, "Papa Mouse made it all up." What else could he have said instead? What would you do if you were one of the mole babies?

For Children Ages 8–12, Relating to "The Wise Hen"
The title of the tale is "The Wise Hen." Do you agree with the title?

Is the world of the hens different from the world of the swifts? Explain how and why.

For which hens were the south and the sea more important? Is what you can't see or don't know important or not? Why or why not?

The hens only believe what one of them has seen. What do you think about that? What would happen if one of the hens said, "I believe the swifts"? What would you do if you were one of the hens?

Has someone ever told you a story that was not true and let you believe it was true? How did you feel about that?

Can you think of a different title for the story?

Little Hamster Never-Enough

by Nel de Theije-Avontuur

Sniff…sniff…snuffle…snuffle. That's what hamsters do all night long to find food.

"At night?" you might wonder.

Yes, because hamsters mostly sleep during the day. Most hamsters, that is, except for Little Hamster Never-Enough. She often snuffled around both night and day, sniffing and snuffling for anything edible.

"Is that so Little Hamster Never-Enough can eat some tasty treats?" wondered Guinea Pig Sunny-Man who lived next to Little Hamster Never-Enough. Often, as he lay in the sun, he wondered what Little Hamster Never-Enough was doing. Mostly he only saw her store her finds. For sure, she stored much more than she ate.

Well, Guinea Pig Sunny-Man just didn't understand it. "What are you doing all the time?" he finally asked her one day.

"Imcllctingfud," came the answer.

"I don't understand a word you are saying!" said Guinea Pig Sunny-Man. It was impossible to understand her because hamsters can't talk so well with a mouth full of food. And they keep putting food in their mouths until their cheeks are bulging.

At that moment, Little Hamster Never-Enough had big fat cheeks. She had to store her food before she could answer. "Well, I'm collecting food," she said at last. "I collect as much food as I can find so I never go hungry. And after that, I collect some more and then some more. Because you never know."

She stopped and looked at Guinea Pig Sunny-Man. "I never see you collecting *any* food," she said to him. "All you do is sit in the sun being lazy. Don't you know that you have to find the perfect spot to store your food?"

"And what then?" asked the guinea pig.

"Then you hide your food."

"And what then?" the guinea pig repeated.

"Then you collect and hide more food!"

"And then what?" the guinea pig asked again.

Little Hamster Never-Enough looked puzzled. It was as if he had not understood a single word she had said. "After I have worked very, very hard and collected and stored a lot of food, I can finally enjoy myself. I will happily sit and laze in the sun."

"Why don't you do that right now? Why don't you join me in the sun?" asked Guinea Pig Sunny-Man.

Contentment

by Erich Kaniok

A rich factory owner saw a fisherman lying next to his boat and smoking a pipe. He didn't understand the fisherman's lazy behavior. Slowly getting annoyed, he asked the fisherman: "Why are you not fishing?"

"Because I already caught enough fish for today," answered the fisherman.

"Why don't you catch some more?"

"What should I do with the fish?"

"You could earn more money," said the factory owner. "With the extra money, you can have an engine installed on your boat. You could sail farther into sea and catch a lot more fish. Then you can earn more money to buy better fishing nets. With them you can catch even more fish and earn even more money. Very soon you will be able to buy two boats...maybe a few more or maybe even a whole fleet. You could be a rich man, just like me."

"And what should I do then?"

"You could really enjoy your life."

"And what do you think I'm doing right now?" asked the fisherman.

DISCUSSION

◉ The Stories

"The Bear and the Piglet," by Max Velthuijs (see References), is a story with a similar theme suitable for children ages 4–6.

"Little Hamster Never-Enough" is suitable for children ages 6–8.

"Contentment" is suitable for children ages 8–12.

◉ Central Theme

Contentment. Learning to be happy and understanding that more doesn't make you a happier person.

◉ Underlying Theme

Learning to consider another's viewpoint.

◉ Developmental Concepts

Dealing with your own feelings of being happy or unhappy. Dealing with contrasts in interests, opinions, and feelings.

Community, norms, and values: Thinking about your workload. Realizing that work is important but so is relaxation.

◉ Open Questions and Guidelines

For Children Ages 6–8, Relating to "Little Hamster Never-Enough"

Will Little Hamster Never-Enough ever be happy? What do you think?

Will she ever have enough food? Little Hamster Never-Enough thinks the guinea pig is lazy. What do you think? Who do you want to be—the hamster or the guinea pig? Explain why.

Do you think the hamster and the guinea pig understand each other? Do you think they'll sit in the sun together or will they do something different? If so what will they do and why?

For Children Ages 8–10, Relating to "Contentment"

Do you think the factory owner is happy with what he has? What do you think and why?

If you could choose, who would you be—the factory owner or the fisherman? Explain your choice.

Do you think the factory owner understands what the fisherman is trying to tell him? What do you think the fisherman is trying to say?

When are you happy or unhappy? Can you explain why?

For Children Ages 10–12, Relating to "Contentment"

Who do you think is happiest, the fisherman or the factory owner? Who would you like to be? Explain your choice.

What reaction do you think the factory owner will have to the fisherman's remark: "And what do you think I'm doing right now?"

Can you think of a time when you were very unhappy? Explain why. Can you think of a time when you were very happy? Explain why.

The King Who Wanted to Touch the Moon

(Adapted by Nel de Theije-Avontuur from
Magical Tales from Many Lands *by Margaret Mayo)*

There was once a king who wanted to have his own way. Everyone had to do what he said—right now!

One cloudless night, he was looking out of the window. Seeing the moon, he decided he wanted to touch it. He reached out his arm again and again with no luck. No matter how far he stretched, he couldn't get near it.

"I can't believe that it's not possible," he said to himself. "I want, I will, I've *got* to touch the moon!"

He thought and thought and suddenly had an idea. He called the best carpenter in the kingdom to his palace and told him to build a tower. "I want a tower so high that I can touch the moon!" the king declared.

The carpenter shook his head. "Your majesty, that is impossible!"

"Nothing is impossible," said the king. "I want you to come to me tomorrow to tell me how you're going to do it."

The carpenter didn't sleep at all that night. He kept thinking that building the tower that the king wanted was just not possible. But he also knew that he'd better do what the king asked if he didn't want to be punished.

Soon it was morning, and the carpenter appeared before the king. "Your majesty," the carpenter said, "the best way to build a very high tower is to stack very strong boxes one on top of the other—hundreds and thousands of boxes—until you reach the sky."

"Very well," said the king. "Let everyone bring all of the strong boxes they have and stack them up." It happened, just as the king wanted, but when

*"I want a tower so high that
I can touch the moon!" the king declared.*

all the boxes had been used, the top of the tower was still nowhere near the moon—it wasn't even as high as the clouds.

"Let everyone bring all the timber there is and make more boxes," said the king. And again, that's just what they did, but still the tower did not reach as high as the clouds.

"There's no timber left," said the carpenter to the king.

"Then chop down all the trees in the kingdom!" ordered the king.

"Your Majesty—we couldn't do that!"

"Whatever I want can be done!" shouted the king angrily.

The distraught carpenter now had all the trees felled and made planks from them to make yet more boxes and piled them higher and higher. When there was no more timber anywhere in the whole kingdom, he told the king that the tower was finished.

That same evening when the moon was high in the sky, the king climbed up higher and higher until he reached the top of the tower and…he still couldn't reach the moon. He stretched himself as tall as he possibly could and reached out and thought that he could *almost* touch it. He called out, "Bring me just one more box, then I'll be able to reach it."

"There aren't any more boxes!" shouted the carpenter.

"Then take the bottom box and bring it up here!"

"Yes, but if I do that…"

"Do what I tell you!" screamed the king from the top of the tower and stamped his foot so hard that the whole tower trembled.

[NOTE TO THE LEADER: *You might ask the children, "How will this story continue?" "What will happen?" And especially—"Why?"*

The end of the story as it is usually told is below.]

The carpenter had no option but to do what the king commanded. He took the first box from the bottom of the tower and ran for his life. And the king? He fell all the way to the bottom, and all the boxes fell down on top of him.

DISCUSSION

◉ **The Story**

"The King Who Wanted to Touch the Moon" is suitable for children ages 6–12.

If you illustrate the story with boxes and puppets, it can also be suitable for children ages 4–6.

◉ **Central Themes**

Selfishness. Insisting on having things your own way. Wanting something and demanding it from others.

◉ **Underlying Themes**

Letting someone have his or her own way. Choosing under the pressure of consequences.

◉ **Developmental Concepts**

Self-awareness: Dealing with your own desires and those of others.

Exercising authority or "playing the boss."

Arguments: Considering when it is a good idea to argue with another person.

◉ **Open Questions and Guidelines**

For Children Ages 6–8

How do you think the story will end? Will the carpenter pull out the bottom box?

If so, why? What do you think of that? If you think he won't do it, why not and what do you think of that decision?

How will things develop between the king and the carpenter if the carpenter decides not to pull out the bottom box? What will happen if he *does* pull out the bottom box?

What do you think of the king? What would you have done if you had been the king?

What do you think of the carpenter? What would you have done if you had been the carpenter?

For Children Ages 8–10

What do you think the carpenter will do? Will he pull out the bottom box? Why or why not? If so, what will happen next?

Did the carpenter know what would happen?

What would you have done if you had been the carpenter? Why?

Did the king not know what would happen if the carpenter pulled the bottom box out? If he might have known it, why didn't he think of that?

What do you think of the king? Why?

For Children Ages 10–12

Why do you think it is that the king thought that it was quite normal for everyone to do what he wanted?

How did it come about that the carpenter thought he should do everything the king asked him to do?

Do you sometimes think that something has to happen because you want it, even if other people don't agree? How do you react when that is done or isn't done?

How do you deal with it when you really want something and need other people to help you accomplish it?

Do you sometimes do something for another person because that person wants it even if you don't agree with it? What do you think of the other person and what do you think of yourself in such a situation?

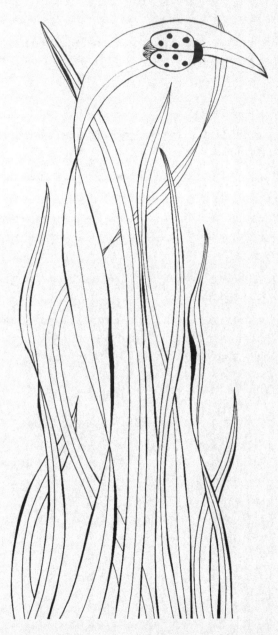

The donkey made fun of the ladybug:
"You're carrying on as if you had climbed a mountain.
It was only a blade of grass!"

The Ladybug and the Lion

by Erich Kaniok

A little ladybug was sitting in the grass. It looked up through the blades of grass and saw the sunshine. "I really fancy some sunbathing," thought the ladybug. "Well, let's start climbing then!" And it started to climb up a blade of grass.

The ladybug was making good progress, and all was going well, until… she fell to the ground and landed on her back. It is very difficult for ladybugs to get upright again, but she managed to turn over and bravely start climbing again. But over and over again, she fell to the ground. Each time, the ladybug looked up to the sunshine and thought: "I will not give up!"

Finally the ladybug reached the sunshine. She felt tired but was proud of herself. She had not given up, and she had not needed any help. She opened up the little wing cases on her back, unfolded her wings, and warmed herself in the sun. It felt amazing, and the ladybug was happy.

Just then, a donkey and an old lion came strolling past. The donkey made fun of the ladybug: "You're carrying on as if you had climbed a mountain," the donkey laughed at the ladybug. "It was only a blade of grass!"

But the lion looked at the ladybug enjoying herself and said, "Well done, little beetle. Enjoy yourself up there. You have achieved what you set out to do. Not all of us have that determination."

DISCUSSION

◉ **The Story**

"The Ladybug and the Lion" is suitable for children ages 6–10.

◉ **Central Themes**

Having the courage and power that is necessary to reach the goal you have chosen.

Having respect for others.

◉ **Underlying Themes**

Having a goal and persisting until you reach it.

Valuing what someone else has achieved in his own way.

Understanding that what is very easy for one person may be a huge achievement for someone else.

◉ **Developmental Concepts**

Self-awareness: Developing one's own capabilities.

Community, norms, and values: Being aware of the capabilities of others and valuing their efforts. Bearing in mind the feelings of others.

Having respect for others. Noticing and appreciating differences.

◉ **Open Questions and Guidelines**

For Children Ages 6–8

Why does the ladybug keep on trying to climb the blade of grass?

What do you think of the donkey? How would you feel if someone laughed at what you had done?

What do you think of the lion?

Have you ever been proud of yourself? Has someone ever been proud of you?

What would you have said to the beetle?

For Children Ages 8–10

Begin with the questions that were used with children ages 6–8 and then add these:

Do you think you also would have kept on trying to climb the blade of grass? Why or why not?

What do you find difficult but still worth trying?

Why do you think the donkey reacted that way to the ladybug? How do you think he would have felt if someone had said such things to him?

Why does the lion react differently? He says, "You have achieved what you set out to do. Not all of us have that determination." What does he mean by that? Have you ever had to put a lot of effort into something to reach your goal? Why did you do it? How did other people react to your accomplishment? How did you want other people to react?

How do you react to other people's achievements even when it might be something you can do with very little effort?

The Millipede

by Nel de Theije-Avontuur

Now, first of all, the name *millipede* is a bit of an exaggeration. This little animal has a great many legs, it's true—thirty, a hundred, maybe even two hundred, but a thousand? You can imagine right away what kind of creature this is: a braggart. That's not true of all of them of course, but the one in this story was.

The millipede in this story was very handsome. He was a lovely orange, had fifteen legs on each side of his body, and had a beautiful head with strong jaws with which to catch his prey—other small creatures—and eat them.

The other millipedes all wanted to look like him, and they often imitated what he did. Our little millipede knew this—he thought himself the best-looking and cleverest of all the millipedes. So one day he thought up something new. "I'm going to do things differently," he said. "I'm done with all that creeping around on all these legs. I'm not going to do that any more. I'm going to walk upright. No more chasing those small creatures we hunt under stones, under twigs, and under the sand! Surely some of them must live out in the open, and I will hunt them. Besides, I'll have quite enough legs to walk upright using just two. And it looks so much cooler."

And so the millipede walked, on two legs, tall and upright.

"Wow," thought the other millipedes. "That looks great. He's so clever." And soon they were all walking on two legs.

Did I say all of the millipedes did this? Well, there was one millipede who didn't. He went on using all of his legs to walk, which allowed him to disappear under piles of stones in search of prey. With so many of the other millipedes walking upright, he had very little competition for food now and often ate until he couldn't eat any more—even as the other millipedes went hungry.

For although our upright millipede was right about finding some prey out in the open, he and the other upright millipedes didn't find a lot. They now had to search longer for food, and it made them all very hungry. They even started fighting with each other over food. And they were also discovering that walking upright made the two feet they used to walk very sore.

Seeing this, the one millipede who had remained on all his legs would sometimes come out from under the stones and shout, "Hey! There's more than enough food here for you. If you walk on all your legs, you'll be able to reach it and catch it."

[NOTE TO THE LEADER: *You can break here to discuss how the story might continue. You might ask, "What do you think the millipedes will do now?" The story continues below.*]

And what do you think? Did they go back to walking on all their legs so they could get under the stones? No! They didn't. They didn't listen and instead hobbled on with their painful feet.

"Well," thought the millipede, watching from the pile of stones, "I want nothing to do with these two-leggers." And with that he disappeared under the stones again.

The Royal Calf

by Erich Kaniok

A king was given a very special calf as a gift. The calf was black as pitch and had not a single white hair. But what was even more interesting about this calf was that it didn't like eating grass. Everyone agreed that was very odd.

The king wanted the calf to have special treatment, so he appointed someone to care for it. The caregiver had to watch the calf all day long and offer him the very best food. But the calf wouldn't eat, and the caregiver was in despair. That is until one day when he watched the calf pick a single piece of clover from an entire stand of clover and take it in his mouth. The caregiver

A king was given a very special calf as a gift.

quickly looked into the royal calf's mouth, and there on his tongue was a four-leaf clover. So that was another peculiarity of this jet-black calf: It only ate four-leaf clovers!

The king was proud of his special calf. In all the cities and villages in the kingdom, posters were hung, calling on all the people to collect four-leaf clovers for the royal calf. It wasn't long before all of the king's subjects were crawling through the fields, along the roadsides, and through their own gardens. They crawled everywhere for the king and his calf. But four-leaf clovers are very rare.

In the kingdom was a man who was very wise and clever. He had come from a distant country. He behaved as though the posters were not addressed to him, and he stood tall and didn't crawl around like everyone else. Instead he watched and listened. Then, when he heard people cry out, "Hooray for the king and his calf," he knew that someone had found a four-leaf clover. He would ask the person to show him where he had found the clover, and then the wise man would dig up the plant, roots and all. He then would take the plant to the clover field he had sown, and start new plants. In this way, the man knew that he would have many four-leaf clovers the following year.

Meanwhile, because the kingdom's population was crawling and searching, they managed to collect enough four-leaf clovers so that the calf not only remained alive, but he also flourished. The people even managed to find enough so that they could dry some to keep the calf eating through winter.

But this situation was not without problems. The trouble was that apart from the king (who naturally did not crawl), and the stranger (who didn't appear to know he should), no one could walk upright anymore. And the people began to think that was normal. As well, the kingdom had become poorer, as of late, since the people had little time for anything but searching for the elusive four-leaf clovers. Finally everyone saw how bad things had become—everyone, that is, except for the king, who saw only his lovely calf.

Then there was the stranger, who had never crawled around but had cultivated a clover plantation that yielded only four-leaf clovers. His field was large enough to feed the calf all through the next summer and even the following winter as well. The people, who hadn't seen anything the stranger was doing in his fields because they had been too busy crawling about, were astonished when, early in the spring, the stranger delivered a couple of months' worth of clover to the court with the message that, from now on, no one needed to crawl around and the people would have time for other, more important things.

Now you might think that the king and the people would be very pleased about all of this. For a while it seemed that they were. They even seemed pleased with the stranger and asked how he got all those four-leaf clovers. Happily, he explained how he did it, saying that it was really not difficult.

But eventually, the people found the stranger's ways hard to accept. "He's not one of us," someone said. "What he says can't be true. It can't be right."

And they decided to continue crawling around looking for four-leaf clovers, which had become almost second nature to them. The king saw this and was proud of his subjects who worked so hard for him and the royal calf. He even told the stranger that he didn't need his clovers, and in the middle of the night two of the best crawlers destroyed his clover plantation. After that, the stranger left the country and the subjects chorused, "Long live the king. Long live his calf!" even as they crawled and searched and hunted for the elusive four-leaf clovers.

DISCUSSION

◉ The Stories

"The Emperor's New Clothes," by Hans Christian Andersen (see References), is a story with a comparable theme for children ages 4–6.

"The Millipede" is suitable for children ages 6–8.

"The Royal Calf" is suitable for children ages 8–12.

◉ Central Themes

Doing what other people tell you without thinking for yourself. Never letting go of learned or prescribed behavior even if it is stupid or senseless.

Not wanting or not being able to change. Ignoring the wisdom of others.

◉ Underlying Theme

Making an idol of a person or object and giving up everything—even important things—for that idol.

◉ Developmental Concepts

Imitating other people instead of developing your own personal characteristics and skills. Exploring change. Considering dependence vs. independence.

Crowd/group behavior: Being critical or open to other people's ideas.

◉ Open Questions and Guidelines

For Children Ages 6–8, Relating to "The Millipede"

What do you think of the millipede who walked on two legs? Why?

What do you think of all the other millipedes who copied him? Why?

Would you rather be like the "cool" millipede and the others who copied him or the one who didn't? Why?

Do you sometimes want to be like someone else? Why? Do you want to copy them?

One of the millipedes goes away because he doesn't want anything more to do with the "two-leggers." Would you have done that?

For Children Ages 8–10, Relating to "The Royal Calf"

What do you think of the king? Why?

All of the king's subjects went on their hands and knees to look for four-leaf clovers. Would you have done that? Why or why not?

The wise stranger says, "Now you have time for more important things." What do you think he meant?

Why didn't the people pay attention to the stranger's words? What do you think of that?

The stranger left. Would you have done that? If not, what would you have done?

Do you sometimes do something because other people think that you should do it? What? Would you actually like to do it differently? How?

For Children Ages 10–12, Relating to "The Royal Calf"

What do you think of the way the king treated the calf?

He asks all of his subjects to crawl around looking for four-leaf clovers. What do you think of that?

Why do all the subjects do that? Why do they continue to do it after the stranger tells them that it's not necessary?

What other things do you think the people should have spent more time on?

What do you think of the stranger? What do you think of his departure? What would you have done?

Do you sometimes see people doing what other people tell them without thinking about it?

Do you see yourself doing that? What things? Could you do something else? How? Would you like to do it differently? Why or why not?

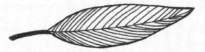

The Hissing Snake

by Erich Kaniok

"Sssssssssssssss!" From out of the high grass in a field of wheat darted a poisonous snake. She was angry! She raised her head, mouth wide open, showing her poisonous fangs and flicking her tongue.

The local shepherds who let their animals graze nearby couldn't get away quickly enough. They were terrified because they knew that the bite of this snake could make people very, very sick or even kill them.

A little way up the road, the shepherds saw a stranger wandering along. They greeted him and warned him about the snake they had seen. To their astonishment, the stranger returned their greeting and continued on his way, undisturbed. No sooner had he reached the path that led by the wheat field, than the snake shot forward, hissing and threatening to bite him.

And then something happened that the snake had never experienced before. The man didn't scream or shout, and he didn't jump out of his skin or run away. He was not frightened at all. He looked at the snake with a friendly smile, and it completely confused her. She stopped hissing and coiled herself back to the ground.

"Why do you make people afraid?" the stranger asked her. "Do you want to bite them, hurt them, or even kill them? It looks as if you do, although you may not realize what you are doing when you are so angry. Now that your anger has cooled off, you are much quieter. Does that feel better?"

The snake couldn't answer anything except a quiet, "Yes."

"The same is true of all living beings: If you are angry or want to do harm, you feel horrible inside."

The snake recognized that feeling all too well.

"When you try to do good, you feel good as well."

"I'd love to believe that," said the snake. "It sounds hard, but I will try it."

The stranger wished her well, promised to return, said goodbye, and walked on. The snake thought she had understood what the man had told her. From now on, she would be friendly toward everyone. She tried not to look like the poisonous snake she was.

The shepherds who had been so afraid of her, discovered that she no longer attacked. They no longer went to pains to avoid her. In fact, remembering how often she had frightened them, they started teasing and even bullying her. And finally one day, because she did nothing to defend herself, they began hitting her with sticks until she didn't move any more. "She's dead," they said to each other and left her lying on the path.

But she wasn't dead. In the cool of the night, she regained consciousness and dragged herself back to her hole. She lay there for several days eating a few leaves that she found close by. Her wounds healed, but she was very thin.

About then, the stranger came wandering through the fields, looking for the snake. He asked the shepherds if they knew where she was. They told him she was dead, but the stranger didn't believe it. When the shepherds had gone home, he called her, and she came out of her hiding place.

"How are you?" he asked.

"I'm much calmer now," she answered.

"But why are you so thin?"

"I've eaten only leaves for a while. I can't kill animals any more. Maybe that's why."

The man shook his head. "That can't be the only reason. Your body is covered in scars. What happened?"

Then the snake told him what had happened; that she hadn't attacked the shepherds because she had learned not to hurt people.

"But, snake," said the man, "you have shown that you don't burst out in anger for anything anymore, and that you don't want to hurt people, but there's one thing you didn't understand."

[NOTE TO THE LEADER: *What did the snake not understand? Discuss this with the children. The questions and guidelines that follow also will give the children plenty of room for their own thoughts and ideas, and they will also see many different ideas come up. If you choose not to stop here, the story continues below.*]

He went on: "We talked about attacking people at random, about biting them. I didn't say anything about hissing. You are a snake, and you will always be a snake. In an emergency, you have to defend yourself. You can raise your head threateningly and hiss, and people will be scared. Just don't do more than that."

The stranger wished her good luck and went on his way again. The snake lay there thinking about what he had said when the shepherds came back along the path. When they saw that she was still alive, they wanted to kill her once and for all. They grabbed sticks and approached her. The snake waited until they were very close, then raised herself as high as she could, showed her fangs, flicked her tongue, and hissed, "Ssssssssssssss!"

The shepherds didn't know what was happening and ran off as fast as their legs could carry them. After that, they always took great pains to avoid the place where the snake lived and thought that this was the reason why no one was ever bitten again. And the snake…she never needed to hide any more.

DISCUSSION

◉ **The Story**

"The Hissing Snake" is suitable for children ages 8–12.

◉ **Central Themes**

Violence: Examining the impulse to hurt people.

Self-defense: Standing up for yourself. Understanding when standing up for yourself becomes aggression.

◉ **Underlying Theme**

Understanding that the way you look at the world and at other people determines how you deal with them and how people react to you.

◉ **Developmental Concepts**

Taking care of your physical and mental health and that of those around you.

Self-awareness: Standing up for yourself.

Conflicts: Avoiding, causing, and resolving. Teasing in group situations. Respecting one another.

This story has its origins in Buddhism, one key aspect of which is peaceful co-existence.

◉ Open Questions and Guidelines

What did the snake not understand about what the stranger had told her?

In the beginning, why did the snake attack the shepherds?

What upset the snake so much? Why?

Do you recognize that feeling—that sometimes you are so mad you just don't know what you're doing? What is another way you could deal with that?

When the shepherds discovered that the snake didn't attack them, they almost beat her to death. What do you think of that?

The snake chose to only eat leaves. Why? What do you think about that?

Why did the snake try not to act like the snake she once was?

[*The following questions can be used once the rest of the story has been told.*]

What did the stranger mean when he said, "You are a snake, and you will always be a snake"?

Why did the snake not bite the shepherds anymore?

After talking with the stranger a second time, the snake didn't need to hide any more. Why? What did she know then?

Do you know when and how to defend yourself? How does that work for you?

Light Goes with You

by Nel de Theije-Avontuur

One cold winter evening, a woman asked her young niece to take bread to a family who lived deep in the forest. It was a gift for the parents of a newborn baby.

"But, Auntie, it is so cold, and it's very far away," said the child.

"Come along. Wrap up warm and think how happy they will be when you get there," her aunt encouraged her.

"Yes, I'm sure they will, but it's already dark outside!" protested the girl.

"Then I'll give you a lamp to take with you. All right?"

"All right," said the girl. Once she was warmly dressed, she took the bread under one arm and the lamp in the other, and off she went. The first part of the trip was easy; the light from the houses along the road cheered her. But the road soon gave way to a path lined with trees instead of houses. The girl walked slowly and more slowly until she finally stood still. She didn't want to turn around, but she was afraid to go on. After she had stood there a while, someone came out of the forest—it was the baby's father!

"Why are you standing there?" he called to her.

"I was on my way to bring you something, but I was afraid to go any farther. It's so dark along there," said the child, pointing forward into the darkness.

"That's true," said the father. "But try this: take one step forward. Where is it dark now?"

"A little bit farther on," answered the girl.

"Take two steps forward. Where is it dark now?"

"A bit farther on," the girl answered.

"When you have light, it goes with you," said the man. "I have to go for a moment, but you can wait here for me, and we can walk on together."

But the girl didn't hear the last part because she was lost in her game of taking steps forward. Three, four, more…and soon she came to the house where the mother and baby were.

When the father came back to the spot where he'd left the girl, he found no one. He hurried back to his house where he found his family and the little girl with the bread, the lamp, and great joy.

Another version of this story is below.

Light Always Shines Ahead

by Erich Kaniok and Leo Kaniok

Once there was a little boy who had to walk a long way in the dark to get to his grandpa's house. He took a flashlight and left the house. Before long, the flashlight wasn't shining very brightly, and it was growing pitch dark around him. The boy looked at the flickering flashlight sadly. "How am I ever going to find my way in the dark?" he said aloud to himself.

Fortunately an old farmer came along the path at that moment and asked the boy why he was walking so hesitantly. The boy told the farmer that he was afraid of walking in the dark with a flashlight that lit the path only two yards ahead of him.

The farmer smiled and said to the boy, "The light also goes a step further each time you walk forward. The light will always be shining two yards ahead of you, so you don't need to worry. You can safely go on your way."

The boy thanked the farmer, thought a minute, and then continued on his way, keeping the farmer's words in mind. And that's how he arrived safely at his grandpa's house—just two yards and a few steps behind the light of his flashlight.

DISCUSSION

◉ **The Stories**

"Light Goes with You" is suitable for children ages 6–12.

"Light Always Shines Ahead" is suitable for children ages 8–12.

◉ **Central Themes**

Fear and trust: Conquering fears.

Accepting help from another person.

◉ **Underlying Theme**

Light and dark in a person's life: Thinking about who or what makes life "darker" or "lighter."

◉ **Developmental Concepts**

Dealing with difficult situations and with fear. Learning to trust.

Accepting help from another person. Offering help.

Enjoying beautiful "light" moments.

◉ **Open Questions and Guidelines**

For Children Ages 6–8, Relating to "Light Goes with You"
What is the little girl afraid of? Why?

What makes the girl less afraid?

Are you sometimes afraid? Does fear keep you from doing something you would actually like to do?

What would help you conquer your fear?

How do you think the girl felt when she reached the family's house?

For Children Ages 8–10, Relating to Either Story
Begin with the questions that were used with children ages 6–8 and then add these:

You may be afraid of something that another person is not at all afraid of. How can that be? Do you have an example?

What helps you when you are afraid? What doesn't help when you are afraid; what makes your fear worse?

Can you think of some way in which a situation that makes you afraid can become "lighter"?

When you feel good, do you feel "light"?

For Children Ages 10–12, Relating to Either Story

Sometimes we have "darkness" in our lives, and that can feel bad for a while. Can you imagine that? Have you experienced it yourself? Did the feeling of darkness pass eventually?

What made that situation "lighter"? Has someone or something helped you in a situation in which you felt "darkness"?

Could you help someone who is having a hard time? How? Can you give an example?

What can you do? What can't you do?

When was or is it "light" in your life?

Buried Treasure

(Adapted by Nel de Theije-Avontuur from
Stories from Around the World *by Heather Amery)*

One evening two old friends, Bruno and Giovanni, were sitting on a bench outside the farm, drinking a glass of wine. They had been chatting for a while when Giovanni suddenly said "Bruno, I think you've got something on your mind."

"That's true," said Bruno. "I'm worried about my grandson Mario. He's a nice enough kid, but he's lazy. He lies about in his hammock doing nothing. I don't know what to do with him."

"Do you think he'd like a couple of gold pieces?" asked Giovanni. "Listen," and he told Bruno his plan.

Grandpa Bruno had to laugh. "It's a great idea," he said. "Let's do it!"

The next morning when Bruno's grandson was lolling about in his hammock enjoying the sunshine, Giovanni wandered over to him. He took a crumpled piece of paper from his pocket, studied it intently, and said, "Mario, I've found an old map. It's a bit hard to read, but if I'm right, it looks as though there are fifty gold pieces buried in that field."

Mario sat up. "Fifty gold pieces! Wow, I want those!" he said. "I'm going to look for them." He jumped out of the hammock and rushed over to the field, which was overgrown with weeds.

"Well, okay, but you'll have to clear the weeds before you start digging."

Mario started right away. When Giovanni came to the field the next morning, Mario was digging. The ground was very dry, so as he dug he created great clouds of dust.

"I think you should dampen the soil so it doesn't make all that dust," said Giovanni. Mario dashed back to the farm to fetch the hose and then he worked on—watering, digging, watering, digging. Much later he looked up and saw a group of schoolchildren watching him.

Mario couldn't believe his eyes.
The entire field was full of lettuce.

"What should I do to make sure that they don't start looking for the treasure?" he asked Giovanni.

"Hmm, if I were you, I'd spread manure over the field. Then they'll lose interest."

Mario ran back to the farm and came back with a wheelbarrow full of horse dung. And he continued: water, dig, manure, water, dig, manure.... By the end of the day, Mario had dug over the entire field, watered it, and spread manure over it. But he hadn't found a single gold piece. He was pretty upset about that and walked back to the farm looking for his grandpa. He didn't notice that as soon as he was gone, Giovanni went out and sowed seeds all over the field before following him back to the farm.

"Maybe I read the map wrong," he said to Mario. "I'll take another look at it. If I find something, I'll let you know."

Mario waited to hear from Giovanni; a week, another week, a couple more weeks passed. Finally Giovanni invited Mario and his grandfather to meet him at the field. When they got there, Mario couldn't believe his eyes. The entire field was full of lettuce.

"You see what can grow because you cleared the field, watered it, dug it over, and fertilized it?" Giovanni smiled.

Mario was just staring at the plants in amazement when a merchant came along. "Those plants look really good," said the merchant. "I'll give you fifty pieces of gold for all of it."

"Done!" said Bruno, and together he, Giovanni, and Mario cut the plants and loaded the merchant's cart. The man paid Bruno and went on his way.

Bruno looked at Mario and handed him the money. "Here! This is for you. You earned it!" Giovanni just stood there laughing.

And from then on, Mario was eager to help his grandfather on the farm, and he learned how to grow all kinds of vegetables to sell.

DISCUSSION

◉ **The Story**

The Little Red Hen, by Max Velthuijs (see References), is a story with a similar theme for children ages 4–8.

"Buried Treasure" is suitable for children ages 8–12.

Central Themes

Sowing in order to harvest—literally and metaphorically.

Finding reward through hard work. Wishes coming true by doing something to make them happen.

Underlying Themes

Helping, cooperating.

Developmental Concepts

Healthy behavior: Learning the importance of hard work.

Social-emotional development: Working in a group. Dealing with the times when you don't feel like pitching in.

Community, norms, and values: Assessing your own contribution at home, at school, and in the community. Finding reward through work.

Open Questions and Guidelines

For Children Ages 8–12

Giovanni and Bruno made a plan. Why did the plan work?

Would Mario have done all that digging, watering, and fertilizing if he had known that there was no gold buried but, rather, that he would earn fifty gold pieces by cultivating and selling lettuce? What do you think? Why?

Imagine: You can choose to have someone give you money without you having to do anything or to earn it by doing something. Which would you choose? Why? What kind of a feeling would it give you if you just received money for no reason? And how would it feel if you got it because you earned it? Is it different? Why would that be?

Are there things that you feel you should do for yourself and others—at school or at home? Do you want to do them? Why or why not? Can you give an example?

Maybe you want to give the story a different ending. What kind of an ending would it be? Why?

A bare field can yield something if you do something with it. Can you give examples of what you might do with it that could earn you what you want?

All Quiet in the Forest

by Nel de Theije-Avontuur

No one knows for sure why, after a hard day's work, the birds of the forest sing, or whistle, or twitter, or screech one last song together. Whatever kind of sound they make, it always sounds good when they do it together.

There is *one* bird among them that cannot only sing well but that also has a feel for rhythm, and that is the conductor bird. With any luck, the other birds watch him, and all the members of the bird choir sing in time with each other.

But, of course, there are birds that sometimes prefer their own little voices, so now and then …how shall we put it? It sounds a little…out of tune. Then all the birds look a little sideways at each other. Usually they can laugh about it, and then they all sing together.

Sung, we should say, because on this particular evening not a single bird was singing. What had happened?

That morning, the woodpecker suddenly thought, "What a pity that I screech. The blackbird sings so much more sweetly. I want to sing as well as the blackbird. I'm going to practice all day, and then, this evening, I will be able to sing beautifully. That will be fantastic!"

Meanwhile, the blackbird thought, "The dove makes so much more lovely sounds than I can. I want to coo like a dove. I'm going to try that."

And the dove thought that the robin could chirp best and wanted to do the same. The robin wanted to sing like the finch, the finch like the blue tit, the blue tit like the thrush, and so on.

And so, as evening fell, it was completely quiet in the forest. No one was singing. The conductor bird waved his wing for the birds to begin, but even that didn't help. No bird could sing the other bird's song.

There is one bird among them
who cannot only sing well
but who also has a feel for rhythm.

The forest remained silent for a long time. The birds grew restless, but everyone was afraid to start. Finally, the wren could take it no longer. "Well I'm just happy that I can sing at all," she thought. "I will sing by myself!" and she started to chirp in her own way.

The bird chorus first listened quietly and then, one by one, the other birds started to join in. Each was singing its own song, but they were all singing together. Even the conductor bird sang along, beating time with his wings.

[NOTE TO THE LEADER: *This story was inspired by the following thought: Use the talents you have; the forest would be very quiet if no bird sung his song except for the very best.*]

Dedicated to Henry Van Dyke

DISCUSSION

◉ **The Story**

"All Quiet in the Forest" is suitable for children ages 6–12.

◉ **Central Theme**

Wanting to be like someone else can lead a person to no longer value her- or himself. Learning to become yourself.

◉ **Underlying Themes**

Good cooperation comes from the contribution of what each person can do.

Considering the role of a leader.

◉ **Developmental Concepts**

Social-emotional development: Learning self-respect and self-awareness. Valuing your own unique capabilities. Having a view of your own limitations.

Cooperation in a group.

Leadership.

◉ **Open Questions and Guidelines**

For Children of All Ages

No one knows why the birds sing together in the evening. Do you have an idea why?

Why was it so quiet in the forest on this day?

Why did so many of the birds want to sing like another bird? How did that come about?

What could the conductor have said or done that would have helped? Why do you think it would have helped?

Have you ever thought that someone else can do something "better" than you can do it? At those times, what do you think about what you *are* able to do? How does it feel?

Would it make any difference if someone told you that what you can do is perfectly good enough? Could you tell yourself that? Do you ever say that to a friend?

At the end of the story, all the birds are singing together again. Why? What do you think changed?

They could all have sung their own song alone. What would you have done? Why?

The Toad and the Goldfish

by Erich Kaniok and Leo Kaniok

The water in the pond glistened in the afternoon sun. By the bank, almost hidden under a pair of huge leaves, sat a toad. He was a big, fat, brown toad with warts.

A goldfish was swimming in the water nearby. "Do you see how beautiful I am?" bubbled the fish. She made a lovely swoosh with her tail.

The toad said...nothing at all. He just looked at her anxiously.

"I understand why you don't say anything," bubbled the goldfish again. "You are a toad. You look like a brown frog, but even a frog is better looking than you are. Look at me! I dance and dart through the water. The sun's rays make it look as if I am made of real gold. I am a goldfish!" Still the toad said nothing. He didn't move a muscle.

"Say something!" screamed the goldfish impatiently, thrashing with her tail. But then...she disappeared into the beak of a heron.

"Bye-bye," said the toad.

The Talkative Tortoise

by Erich Kaniok

Somewhere deep in the forest lived a tortoise. He had become friends with two young swans who foraged for food in the water nearby.

One day, the swans said to the tortoise, "Dear tortoise, we enjoy your company so much. Shall we live together forever? We live a little way from here, in a lake in the mountains. It's much more beautiful there than here in your muddy pool. We only come down here to eat, and then we go home. Come with us. You'll enjoy it."

The tortoise shook his head in doubt. "How on earth would I get to the mountains? I can't climb a mountain!"

The swans answered, "We'll take you there. If we fly close together holding a branch in our beaks, and you bite on the branch with your very strong jaws, we can carry you! Of course you'll have to remember not to talk during the journey!"

"That sounds like a great idea," answered the tortoise. "I'll come with you."

Then the swans took a strong branch, the tortoise bit down on it hard, and off they went. The swans flew gently and evenly, and the tortoise found it quite easy to hold on to the branch with his mouth. Together they flew over forests, lakes, and villages, and at last they flew over a palace. The swans flew a little lower there so that the tortoise could see the king's beautiful palace.

Children, hearing the beating of wings in the air, looked up and say "Hey! That's not possible! Look! Two swans are carrying the tortoise. Obviously he can't go where he wants to go by himself." The tortoise was annoyed when he heard that and wanted to shout "Brats!" but as soon as he opened his mouth to shout, he let go of the stick and fell into the courtyard of the palace.

[*NOTE TO THE LEADER: For children ages 8–10, you can end the story here.*]

The guards ran to where the turtle had fallen, and the rumor then spread around the palace like wild-fire, "A tortoise has fallen into the courtyard from the air!"

The king went down with his entourage and saw the dead tortoise lying there. He asked his senior adviser, "How could a tortoise fall into the court-yard?"

The king was asking a question! This was the moment the adviser had been waiting for because the king didn't ask him anything very often. Giving good advice to a king who mostly liked to talk for himself was not an easy task. The adviser said, "Your majesty, when the guards started shout-ing, I saw two swans flying together above the palace. They were carrying a stick between them, held in their beaks. Probably they had the tortoise bite onto the stick so they could carry him somewhere. But because the tortoise couldn't keep his mouth shut, he let go of the stick and fell down. It cost him his life. That's the way it goes, great king."

The king was suspicious. It looked for a moment as if he were going to get angry, but he smiled and said, "I think I see what you mean."

DISCUSSION

◉ **The Stories**

"The Toad and the Goldfish" is suitable for children ages 4–8.

"The Talkative Tortoise" is suitable for children ages 8–12.

◉ **Central Themes**

Talking, listening, being quiet. The dangers of not being able to stay silent.

◉ **Underlying Themes**

The dangers of feeling important.

Listening to or ignoring good advice even if it is given through silence.

◉ **Developmental Concepts**

Internal: Orientation toward self and the world.

Social-emotional development: Self-awareness. Healthy self-appreciation. The danger of excessive self-sufficiency. Being aware of and open to other people.

Healthy behavior: Learning not to ignore personal safety.

Community, norms, and values: Being able to listen also means being open to other peoples' opinions.

⦿ Open Questions and Guidelines

For Children Ages 6–8, Relating to "The Toad and the Goldfish"

What do you think the goldfish wanted to hear from the toad? Do you also sometimes want other people to only look at you?

The toad says nothing, but he looks up anxiously. Why? Do you think the goldfish noticed that he looked up anxiously? No? Why not? Or if she did notice, she ignored the warning. Why?

The goldfish came to a sticky end. How?

"Bye-bye" said the toad. What did he think of the goldfish and what happened to her? What do you think of the goldfish?

For Children Ages 8–10, Relating to the First Part of "The Talkative Tortoise"

The tortoise thought that he would be able to keep his mouth shut. Why did everything go wrong?

Why was the tortoise so annoyed by what the children said? How would you feel if other people thought that you couldn't do something?

For Children Ages 10–12, Relating to the Complete Story of "The Talkative Tortoise"

Have you ever had the feeling that it would be better to say nothing? Why? Did you keep quiet or not? In either case, why?"

This was the moment the senior adviser had been waiting for. Why do you suppose he had to wait so long for that chance?

At first the king was suspicious, almost angry, with the adviser's answer. Why?

The king finally responded, saying, "I think I know what you mean." What was it that he knew?

Do you know a proverb that goes with this story?

Earthworms

by Nel de Theije-Avontuur

Earthworms are really useful. They think so themselves, but many farmers and people with gardens think so, too. Worms are like little underground plows. They keep the soil loose and add their own fertilizer…their poo…to it as well.

Worms are also tasty. They don't think so, but many birds find them to be the absolutely best thing on the menu! Fortunately for worms, birds aren't underground, but now and then a worm wants a bit of air, a drop of rain, a little wind, or a touch of warmth. So our little Wormlet, as we will call him, had decided to go out for a breath of fresh air.

Eating and pooping his way upward, he could feel that he was coming to the surface even though he couldn't see a thing. That meant that he also couldn't see the big fat blackbird sitting on the tree branch overhead. The bird was quietly watching that heap of soil that had just piled up and from which a tasty little worm had just emerged. The bird hopped from the branch onto the ground….

Wormlet felt that, and he immediately said, "Uh-oh! Wrong move!" He wouldn't be able to dive back under the ground fast enough, he knew, but what could he do? In an instant, he had an idea.

"Ah, Mrs. Blackbird," he said. "What a good thing I met you! In my tunnel, I just heard that a whole herd of worms is coming this way. If you come any closer to eat me up, they'll hear you, and they won't come out. If you let me go quietly back into my tunnel, you'll only have to wait a moment, and then you can fill your stomach!"

The blackbird didn't need to think long. She imagined all those worms coming out of the ground, and she let little Wormlet go home without bothering him. And Wormlet? Once he was safely back under the ground, he started to laugh like a…hmmmm, how do worms laugh? Do you know?

"Ah, Mrs. Blackbird," he said.
"What a good thing I met you!"

⦿ **The Story**

"Earthworms" is suitable for children ages 6–10.

⦿ **Central Theme**

Greed and the consequences of greed. Not being content with what you have and always wanting more.

⦿ **Underlying Theme**

How there is more than one way to protect yourself. The worm saved himself by using his smarts.

⦿ **Developmental Concepts**

Healthy behavior: Food—understanding the addictive qualities of something delicious.

Social-emotional development: Seeing and dealing with the idiosyncrasies in your behavior and that of other people.

⦿ **Open Questions and Guidelines**

For Children Ages 6–8

The blackbird ends up with nothing. How did that happen?

What do you think of the fat blackbird? Why?

What do you think of the worm? Why?

For Children Ages 8–10

How would you complete the following sentences:

* "The blackbird is…"   * "The worm is…"

Can you complete the same line about yourself: "I am…." Do you like that about yourself? Why? Maybe you don't like it so much. Why?

The blackbird is greedy. Do you see that characteristic in yourself as well? Do you have other characteristics? Which of your characteristics do you like to have? Do other people around you also find that a good characteristic? Why or why not?

What characteristic are you not happy to have? What do other people think of it? Why?

The worm saves himself by lying.
What do you think about that? Why?

Partridges

by Nel de Theije-Avontuur

This is a story about partridges. What are partridges? Well, they are a bit like small wild chickens that generally live close to wheat or cornfields. Why? Because these areas always have lots of delicious grains of corn and wheat for hungry birds to eat.

Partridges have brown feathers that are almost the same color as the earth in the fields. That coloring allows the birds to be invisible so that the predators—birds, foxes, and other animals including human beings who think partridges are good to eat—can't see them easily.

Because of their many predators, partridges have to be very, very careful. There is always a special partridge, a male bird, who is the leader. He is the boss, and all of the other partridges listen to what he says. If he says, "Karrrrrwik!" it means, "Get away!" Then all the partridges fly off together. They have to practice that sometimes, and that's just what they were doing on this one particular day.

Pecking grains from the field, a group of partridges waited for the leader to call out the command. They would be ready if he called for them to take off fast. At the edge of the field a new partridge had just arrived. He was alone and stood watching the others with their leader. He was sure he could better lead the group, but that would mean getting rid of the existing leader. "Hey, there," he called out to the leader. "I think I'd make a better leader than you. Let's fight to see which one of us is stronger!"

"I've got no time for that sort of thing," said the older partridge. "And I don't want to fight either." He ignored the lone partridge and went back to guarding his flock.

Now the other partridge started to challenge him. "You are afraid to fight me!"

The older partridge didn't respond. He turned his attention to the training, shouting, "Get away!" to the group of birds.

Now the new bird was annoyed and started insulting the leader: "Scaredy-cat partridge! Stupid cock!"

The group stopped practicing and watched to see what the boss bird would do, but he did nothing. The new partridge went on swearing and yelling insults until he was tired out. Then, just as quietly as he'd come, he gave up and flew away.

"Why did you let him say all those nasty things to you like that?" one of the birds asked.

And the older partridge answered, "Sticks and stones...." and added, "Words don't hurt. If I don't take it to heart, it doesn't bother me. Who then does it bother?"

In the Schoolyard

by Nel de Theije-Avontuur

It was recess, and the children were playing outside in the schoolyard. Some children were playing alone. Some were standing around or playing in groups.

One of the groups was playing that they had just arrived in a spaceship and were just discovering this planet called Earth. These explorers found many new and interesting things on Earth, but there were dangers as well. Some people on the new planet wanted to hunt down these visitors from space, with violence if necessary. So the spaceship group was practicing their fighting skills. Bert, one of the bigger children, was the leader. He knew how to fight well and was training the others.

Today a new boy had come to the school. He stood watching the space people practicing and thought, "I could lead that group much better!" He challenged Bert. "You wanna fight with me? Shall we see who's the strongest?"

When Bert didn't react, the new boy was irritated.

"Is that fighting?" he yelled, cursing in between. "Ridiculous! What a stupid fighter you are. You call yourself a man?"

So the new boy went on and on. Bert took no notice and continued playing and leading the others. In the end, the new boy didn't know what to do. He turned on his heels and walked off.

Bert wanted to go on with the practice, but the other children didn't understand. "Why did you let him say all that stuff?" they asked.

"Oh, sticks and stones may break my bones, but words can never hurt me," Bert shrugged. "And cursing doesn't hurt either. If I don't take it to heart, who is it hurting?"

Who Does It Belong To?

by Erich Kaniok and Leo Kaniok

Once there was a very famous warrior. Young people came to him regularly to study with him. One day, a young warrior came to him. He was determined to be the first person to beat the old warrior.

As well as being strong, this young warrior was also cunning and knew how to exploit every weakness his opponent had. It was his habit to wait until the opponent attacked. That way he could see where the other's weakness lay and then he would strike with great speed and power and without mercy. No one lasted very long in a bout with him.

Against the pleas of his concerned young pupils, the old warrior accepted the challenge from the young man. When the two of them stood face to face ready to begin their fight, the young man began insulting the older man, calling him all kinds of bad names. He then started slinging mud at him and spat in his face several times. The young warrior hoped his actions would make the older man attack. He continued with this for quite a while, but the old warrior simply didn't react. When the young man had exhausted himself, he gave up.

In shame, he turned around and left the ring. Upset and disappointed about the fact that the master had allowed himself to be so insulted and belittled in public, the pupils came to him and asked, "How can you just let that happen? Something so humiliating! How could you allow him to say all those things about you?" At first the master was silent and just looked at each of his students one by one. Then he answered, "If someone insults you but you don't react, you don't allow yourself to be insulted. Who is hurt then? If someone wants to give you something, but you don't accept it, who does it belong to?"

DISCUSSION

◉ **The Stories**

The Grouchy Ladybug, by Eric Carle (see References), is a book with a similar theme for children ages 4–6.

"Partridges" is suitable for children ages 6–8.

"In the Schoolyard" is suitable for children ages 8–10.

"Who Does It Belong To?" is suitable for children ages 10–12.

◉ **Central Theme**

Dealing with challenges and insults. The power of not reacting to attacks.

◉ **Underlying Theme**

Making your own choices. The leader doesn't allow himself to be influenced by other people.

◉ **Developmental Concepts**

Social-emotional development: Dealing with conflicts. Self-awareness.

Community, norms, and values: Respecting each other. Reflecting on fights: prevention, causes, resolution. Dealing with group pressure.

◉ **Open Questions and Guidelines**

For Children Ages 6–8, Relating to "Partridges"

What do you think of the new partridge? What do you think of the boss, the cock? Why?

Do you also think that the cock shouldn't let the other bird curse at him? What should he do instead?

What does the leader mean when he says, "sticks and stones..." and "words don't hurt"?

He also says, "When I don't take it to heart it doesn't bother me." Who does it bother in that case?

Do words really not hurt?

Have you ever insulted someone? Why? What happened?

Have you ever been insulted, teased or bullied? How did that feel? What did you do? Why? What happened?

Maybe you could finish this story. What would happen to that new partridge?

Can the leader of the group of birds do anything to help him?

For Children Ages 8–10, Relating to "In the Schoolyard"

What do you think of the new boy? What do you think of Bert?

Are the other children right when they say, "You can't let him talk to you that way?"

What does Bert mean when he says, "sticks and stones" and "cursing doesn't hurt?"

"If I take no notice if it, who does it bother?" he says. What do you think?

Do words really not hurt people?

Have you ever insulted someone? Why? What was the result?

Have you ever been insulted, teased, or bullied? How did that feel? What did you do? Why? What was the result?

Maybe you know how the story will continue. What will happen to the new boy?

Can Bert do anything for him?

For Children Ages 10–12, Relating to "Who Does It Belong To?"

Why do the other students not want the teacher to take on the challenge?

Is the young warrior stronger when he exploits the weaknesses of another person? What do you think?

The older warrior takes no notice of all the insults. What would you have done? Why? Do words really not hurt?

How do you think things went for the young warrior afterward? What would you have done if you had been in his position?

At the end of the story comes the question: "If someone wants to give you something but you don't accept it, who does it belong to?" What is that question about? Can you answer it?

Maybe you can write a follow-up to this story. What does the young warrior do? Can the old warrior do something for him?

*We are and will always
be made of the same water!*

The Little Wave

by Erich Kaniok

A huge wave was rolling over the sea toward the beach. A tiny little wave was rolling in right behind it. It had to work extremely hard to keep up with that big wave.

When the two waves got closer to the beach, the little wave said to the big wave, "You know what's going to happen now? You're going to break with lots of noise and splashing on the beach, and I'm going to come in behind you with a tiny little smack."

"That's the wrong way to look at it," said the big wave.

"But it's true," said the little one. "I'm so teeny weeny. No one will even notice I'm there."

The big wave asked, "Little wave, what are you made of?"

"Water," answered the little wave.

"And what am I made of?"

"Also water," the little wave said.

"Then we're just the same," said the big wave. "We're both made of water. And when we're not waves any more, what will we be?"

"Water," said the little wave, but then he added, "and then?"

"Why do you ask that?" said the big wave. "We are and will always be made of the same water!"

"In that case, big wave, then I know what will happen. Next time I will be bigger than you, and I'll be a huge great tidal wave!"

"Hmmm, yes. Perhaps you will," sighed the big wave.

DISCUSSION

◉ **The Story**

Good Job, Little Bear, by Martin Waddell and Barbara Firth (see References), is a story with a similar theme for children ages 4–6.

"The Little Wave" is suitable for children ages 6–12.

◉ **Central Theme**

Equality: Although the shape is different, in fact the big wave and the little wave are the same. They are both made of water.

◉ **Underlying Themes**

Identity: Learning respect for individuality and your own capabilities.

Self-development.

◉ **Developmental Concepts**

Expressing your feelings, wishes, and opinions. Seeing your own capabilities, characteristics, and limitations.

Seeing equality in spite of differences.

◉ **Open Questions and Guidelines**

For Children Ages 6–8

Why is the little wave sad?

What does the big wave tell him?

Who would you like to be, the big wave or the little wave? Why?

Will the big wave be sad when the little wave grows much, much bigger? What do you think?

For Children Ages 8–10

Do you agree with what the big wave says about the two waves being the same? Why do you agree or disagree?

What would you say or do if you were the big wave?

What would you say or do if you were the little wave?

Would the little wave feel better if he were the big wave? Why?

Have you ever felt very small? How was that?

Have you ever thought, "I wish I were bigger?" When? Why?

For Children Ages 10–12

What does the little wave really find so difficult?

"We're just the same," says the big wave. How are they the same? Do you agree with that idea?

Will the little wave really feel better if he becomes a big tidal wave?

How will the big wave feel then? Why do you think that?

Have you ever felt bigger than someone else? How did that feel?

Have you ever felt smaller than other people? How did that feel?

References

Books and Stories Mentioned in this Book

The Dawn Chorus by Ragnhild Scamell and Judith Riches (ABC/The All Children's Co., 1994).

Duck and the Fox by Max Velthuijs (Hamlyn Young Books, 1987).

Elephant and Crocodile by Max Velthuijs and Anthea Bell (Farrar Straus & Giroux, 1990).

"The Emperor's New Clothes" by Hans Christian Andersen in *The Complete Fairy Tales of Hans Christian Anderson* (Gramercy, 1993).

"The Fisherman and His Wife" by the Brothers Grimm in *The Complete Grimm's Fairy Tales* (Pantheon, 1976).

Good Job, Little Bear by Martin Waddell and Barbara Firth (Candlewick Press, 1999).

The Grouchy Ladybug by Eric Carle (HarperCollins, 1996.)

Little Beaver and the Echo by Amy MacDonald and Sarah Fox-Davies (Candlewick, 1995).

The Little Boy and the Big Fish by Max Velthuijs (North-South Books, 1987).

Little Man Finds a Home by Max Velthuijs (Henry Holt, 1985).

The Little Red Hen by Max Velthuijs (DC Heath and Co, 1989).

Little Turtle and the Song of the Sea by Sheridan Cain and Norma Burgin (Crocodile Books, 2000).

Merry Christmas, Ernest and Celestine by Gabrielle Vincent (William Morrow & Co. Library, 1984).

The Rainbow Fish by Marcus Pfister (North-South Books, 1992).

Rikki by Giudo van Genechten (Clavus Publishing, 2008).

Rosie and Roger by Rik Dessers (Tallfellow Press, 2002).

Stories Taken from Around the World

"The Royal Calf," "Four Words," "The Poor Man and the King," "A Thousand Mirrors," "The Calabash of Rice," "The Hissing Snake," "The Displaced

Eagle," and "Contentment" were adapted from *De taal van de stilte: verhalen en parabels uit Oost & West* [The language of silence: stories and parables from East & West] collected by Erich Kaniok.

"Signs on the Road," "The Tenth Donkey," "The Stonemason," "The Hungry Kaftan," and "The Touchstone" were adapted from *Sleutels tot het hart: verhalen en parabels uit Oost & West* [Keys to the heart: stories and parables from East & West] collected by Erich Kaniok.

"The Five French Fries," "Three Life Questions," "The Cracked Pot," "The Reeds," "The Teacher and the Stones," "The Talkative Tortoise," "The Gardener," "The Little Wave," "The Ladybug and the Lion," and "Two Crooked Bricks" were adapted from *Voorbij de woorden: boeddhistische verhalen en parables* [Beyond the words: Buddhist stories and parables] collected by Erich Kaniok.

"Just One Starfish," "A Single Snowflake," "The Three Frogs," "The Rooster and the Sun," "The Boy and the Seagulls," "The Ant and the Grain of Wheat," "The Bird," "The Wise Hen," "Light Always Shines Ahead," "The Toad and the Goldfish," and "Who Does It Belong To?" were adapted from *Het geluk van Tao: verhalen en parables uit China* [The happiness of Tao: stories and parables from China] collected by Erich Kaniok and Leo Kaniok.

"Buried Treasure" was adapted by Nel de Theije-Avontuur from *Stories from Around the World* by Heather Amery (Educational Development Corporation, 2001).

"The King Who Wanted to Touch the Moon" was adapted by Nel de Theije-Avontuur from *Magical Tales from Many Lands* by Margaret Mayo (Dutton Juvenile, 1993).

"Invisible Hunters" was adapted by Nel de Theije-Avontuur from *De koning en de Indiaan: Verhalen uit Nicaragua* [The king and the Indian: Stories from Nicaragua] by Dick Bloemraad, Susan Breedijk, Fiona Macintosh, and Landelijk Stedenbanden Nederland-Nicaragua (Leopold, 1992).

"All Quiet in the Forest," "A Different Chirp," "Earthworms," "The Five French Fries," "Grandfather Ant and Little Ant," "The Horse's Three Questions," "In the Schoolyard," "Jesse's Pet," "Little Hamster Never-Enough," "The Lucky Nut," "The Millipede," "The Mole and the Mouse," "Partridges," "Light Goes with You," "The Circus Elephant," "The Three Caterpillars," "The Three Kittens," "Two Crooked Boxes," "Two Hedgehogs and One Worm," and "The Young Bird of Prey" are by Nel de Theije-Avontuur.

About the Authors

Nel de Theije-Avontuur is married, the mother of two daughters and a son, and grandmother to four grandchildren.

She worked in the Netherlands as a teacher in different schools and as a kind of social worker: with children in preschool, kindergarten, and elementary school and with adults. For most of her career, she worked at the Mytylschool, a school for children with special needs such as physical disabilities, challenges with learning, emotional and behavioral disorders, and developmental disorders. Working there, she was always looking for stories to help her and the children think about themselves, the events in their lives, and what was important and meaningful.

Inspired by a collection of stories, she began to translate and edit the broad range of stories for the children with whom she worked. Simultaneously, she began to write stories of her own.

Writing stories herself is one the hobbies she likes the most. Asking herself questions is what she does the most!

Leo Kaniok is an associate at ZintenZ, producer and publisher of meaningful media under the motto: practical inspiration and applicable meaning.

He is also creator of the website www.meaningful-stories.com; the stories collected on this site help people find inspiration and meaning in daily life.

Together with Erich Kaniok, father and friend, he has published a number of other story collections through Ashoka Publishing House. And with Pars Fortunae Corporate Stories, ZintenZ also organizes workshops working with stories and metaphors: The power of stories.

For more information, contact Leo Kaniok at leo@zintenz.nl.

Printed in the USA
CPSIA information can be obtained
at www.ICGtesting.com
JSHW022340140824
68134JS00019B/1599